MUSIC OF THE MIDDLE AGES

An Anthology for Performance and Study

DAVID FENWICK WILSON

Translations from the Latin and Italian by
Dr. Robert Crouse

Translations from the French and Provençal by
Dr. Hans T. Runte

SCHIRMER BOOKS
A Division of Macmillan, Inc.
New York
Collier Macmillan Canada
Toronto
Maxwell Macmillan International
New York   Oxford   Singapore   Sydney

Schirmer Books
A Division of Macmillan, Inc.
866 Third Avenue, New York, N.Y. 10022

Collier Macmillan Canada, Inc.
1200 Eglinton Avenue East, Suite 200
Don Mills, Ontario M3C 3N1

Library of Congress Catalog Card Number: 90-39279

Printed in the United States of America

printing number
1 2 3 4 5 6 7 8 9 10

Library of Congress Cataloging-in-Publication Data

Music of the Middle Ages

   Includes English translations.
   Intended for use in conjunction with the text: Music
of the Middle Ages : style and structure / David
Fenwick Wilson. New York : Schirmer Books, c1990.
   Contents: Plainchant — Early organum — Free
organum — [etc.]
   1. Musical analysis—Music collections. 2. Music
appreciation—Music collections. 3. Vocal music—500—
1400. I. Wilson, David Fenwick. II. Wilson, David
Fenwick, Music of the Middle Ages.
MT6.5.M9 1990   90-39279
ISBN 0-02-872952-8

Contents

Preface   xi

PART   1

Plainchant

1

1   Gradual *Viderunt omnes**   2

2   Introit *Resurrexi*   4
    A. Complete chant*
    B. Melodic trope of antiphon*
    C. Textual-melodic trope of antiphon*

3   Communion antiphon *Surrexit Dominus*   8

4   Alleluia: *Angelus domini; Respondens**   9

5   Alleluia: *Adorabo ad templum*   10

6   Offertory *Stetit angelus*   11
    A. Complete chant
    B. Prosula *Stetit Michael*

7   Great Responsory *Aspiciens a longe*   15

8   Tract *Vinea facta est*   18

9   Tract *Laudate Dominum*   20

*Specially recorded for *Recording to Accompany Music of the Middle Ages:* (Schirmer Books), ISBN 0-02-872953-6

10 Kyrie *Clemens Rector* 21
 A. Version of the modern *Graduale Romanum**
 B. Texted version from the twelfth century*

11 Agnus Dei *Redemptor mundi* 26
 A. Version of the modern *Graduale Romanum*
 B. Troped version from the eleventh century

12 Sanctus III 28

13 Gloria IV 29

14 Credo I 31

15 Sequence *Regnantem sempiterna** 34

PART 2

Early Organum

37

16 Examples of Parallel Organum from the *Musica enchiriadis* 38
 A. At the octave
 B. At the fifth
 C. At the fourth
 D. Composite parallel organum at the fifth

17 Examples of Oblique Organum 40
 A. From the *Musica enchiriadis*
 B. From the first Bamberg dialogue
 C. From the first Bamberg dialogue
 D. From the second Bamberg dialogue

18 *Alleluia: Angelus domini; Respondens* (oblique organum)* 42

PART 3

Free Organum

45

19 Cunctipotens genitor Deus (texted Kyrie)   46

20 Alleluia: Justus ut palma*   47

21 Alleluia: O quam pulchra est   48

22 Ut tuo propitiatus (responsory verse)   50

23 Alleluia: Surrexit Christus   51

24 Alleluia: Angelus Domini*   52

25 Dicant nunc Judei (processional antiphon verse)   53

PART 4

Aquitanian Sacred Music

55

26 Congaudeat ecclesia (monophonic versus)*   56

27 Plebs domini (monophonic versus)*   57

28 Letabundi jubilemus (monophonic versus)*   59

29 Novum festum celebremus   61
        A. Monophonic versus*
        B. Polyphonic versus*

30 Orienti oriens (polyphonic versus)*   64

31 Lux refulget (polyphonic versus)   66

32 Nuptialis hodie (polyphonic versus)   68

33 Preconia virginis laudum (respond prose)   70

PART 5

Aquitanian Secular Music

73

---

34 Bernart de Ventadorn, *La dousa votz* (two transmissions) — 74

35 Bertran de Born, *Rassa, tant creis* — 76

36 Arnaut Daniel, *Lo ferm voler** — 79

PART 6

Liber Sancti Jacobi

83

---

37 Master Walter of Castle Renard, *Regi perhennis* (conductus) — 84

38 Master Goslen, *Alleluia: Vocavit Jhesus Jacobum** — 85

PART 7

Parisian Sacred Music

87

---

39 *Alleluia: Adorabo ad templum* (organum duplum, comparative versions)* — 88

40 Perotin, *Alleluia: Posui adiutorium* (organum triplum) — 110

41 *Veste nuptiali* (monophonic conductus simplex)* — 116

42 *O curas hominum* (monophonic conductus cum cauda)* — 118

43 *Omnes gentes* (monophonic rondellus) — 120

44 *Ver pacis aperit* (two-voice conductus simplex)* — 121

45 *Quod promisit ab eterno*
(two-voice conductus cum cauda)   123

46 *A solis ortus cardine* (three-voice conductus
cum cauda)*   128

PART 8

The Early Motet

133

47 *Virgo plena gratie—Go*   134
     A. Source clausula
     B. Single-texted three-voice motet

48 A. *O Maria, maris stella—Veritatem*   139
     (single-texted three-voice motet)*
     B. *O Maria virgo—O Maria, maris stella—Veritatem**
     (double motet)

49 *Quant je parti—Tuo* (two-voice motet)*   144

50 *Veni, virgo—Veni, sancte—Neuma* (double motet)   146

51 *En non Diu—Quant voi—Eius in oriente*
(double motet)*   149

52 *Trop sovent—Brunete—In seculum* (double motet)*   151

PART 9

The Continental Motet in the Late Thirteenth Century

153

53 *Tout solas—Bone amour—Ne me blasmes mie*
(conservative motet on a French tenor)   154

54 *J'ai mis—Je n'en puis—Puerorum*
(Franconian motet)*   157

55 *Amours qui—Solem justicie—Solem*
(Petronian motet)*   163

PART 10

The English Motet

169

56 *Inviolata integra mater*—*Inviolata integra et casta* (troped chant setting in single-texted three-voice motet form)   170

57 *O Maria stella maris*—*Jhesu fili summi*—[Tenor] (double motet)   174

58 W. de Wycombe(?), *Alleluya Christo iubilemus*—*Alleluya: Dies sanctificatus* (troped chant setting)*   177

59 *Dulciflua tua memoria*—*Precipua michi*—*Tenor de Dulciflua* (double motet)   184

60 *Solaris ardor*—*Gregorius sol*—*Petre tua*—*Mariounette douche* (triple motet)   187

61 *Ave miles celestis*—*Ave rex* (voice-exchange motet)*   191

62 *Rosa delectabilis*—[*Regali ex progenie*]—*Regalis exoritur* (duet motet)*   196

PART 11

The Continental Motet in the Fourteenth Century

201

63 Philippe de Vitry, *Tuba sacre*—*In arboris*—*Virgo sum* (isorhythmic motet)   202

64 Guillaume de Machaut, *Quant en moy*—*Amour et biaute*—*Amara valde* (isorhythmic motet)*   206

65 Guillaume de Machaut, *De bon espoir*—*Puis que la douce*—*Speravi* (isorhythmic motet)*   212

66 Anonymous, *A vous, vierge*—*Ad te, virgo*—*Regnum mundi* (isorhythmic motet)   217

67 Anonymous, *Post missarum sollempni—Post missa modulamina—Contratenor—Tenor* (four-voice double motet with alternate solus tenor)   223

PART 12

The Polyphonic Song in France
231

68 Guillaume de Machaut, *Dame, vostre doulze viaire* (virelai)*   232

69 Machaut, *Se je souspir* (virelai)*   235

70 Machaut, *Puis qu'en oubli* (rondeau)*   238

71 Machaut, *Quant je ne voy* (rondeau)*   239

72 Machaut, *Amours me fait desirer* (ballade)*   242

73 Machaut, *Une vipere en cuer* (ballade)   245

74 Machaut, *De toutes flours* (ballade)*   248

75 Jacob Senleches, *Fuions de ci* (ballade in mannerist style)*   251

PART 13

The Polyphonic Song in Italy
255

76 Giovanni da Firenze, *Appress' un fiume* (madrigal)*   256

77 Lorenzo Masini da Firenze, *Sovra la riva* (madrigal)   259

78 Giovanni da Firenze, *Chon brachi assai* (caccia)*   263

79 Francesco Landini, *I' priego amor* (ballata)   268

80 Francesco Landini, *Cara mie donna* (ballata)*   272

Preface

Music of the Middle Ages: An Anthology for Performance and Study, along with its Recordings, is designed to accompany *Music of the Middle Ages: Style and Structure* and to provide basic material for study and performance. It can also serve on its own as an independent anthology of medieval music. In this regard, care has been taken whenever possible to avoid duplication with other published anthologies and to give students and performers a wide range of easily accessible examples of medieval music.

Only complete compositions have been included, and full texts are given for strophic songs. Liturgical settings that are partly polyphonic have been completed by including the appropriate plainchant portions. The one major omission that results from this policy is the exclusion of fourteenth-century polyphonic mass settings, the inclusion of which would have extended the present anthology beyond a practical limit.

Considerable attention is given to the usually neglected early stages of polyphony, for short and seemingly primitive as many of these examples seem, they hold the seeds of all future polyphonic development. The artistic masterpieces of the thirteenth century grew out of the techniques and aesthetics of the eleventh and twelfth, which are themselves only the logical extension, albeit a remarkable one, of the theoretical and practical ideas of the tenth. In truth, some of these earlier miniatures have a charm of their own—consider the grace of the early Chartres examples or the noble simplicity of the polyphonic *Cunctipotens genitor* trope.

The twelfth century is represented on the one hand by the monophonic sacred versus of southern France and the secular monophony of the troubadours and on the other by the sacred polyphony of both southern and northern France through the music of Aquitainia and of the *Liber Sancti Jacobi*. This in turn leads to the treasures of Notre Dame organa and conductus. Particular attention is given to both monophonic and polyphonic conductus, and to the multiple versions of a typical organum setting.

Motet style begins in thirteenth-century France, continues with late thirteenth- and early fourteenth-century English examples, and concludes with the continental isorhythmic motet. The polyphonic song of the fourteenth century encompasses both France and Italy in their most characteristic forms.

Multiple versions of some chant melodies have been included. Troped and nontroped examples are given for several plainchants and one, the *Alleluia: Angelus Domini*, is presented in both medieval plainchant and eleventh- and twelfth-century polyphonic settings. Another, the *Alleluia: Adorabo ad templum*, reappears both in multiple Notre Dame organum duplum versions and, with the alternate text *Alleluia: Posui aduitorium*, as set in three voices by Perotin. Indeed, the Alleluia as a chant forms a touchstone of comparison, being present in numerous examples throughout the period covered by the Anthology.

Transcriptions, unless otherwise acknowledged, have been newly made by the author. In most cases they represent the version of a single medieval manuscript and attempt to convey that particular reading as literally as possible. This extends to the inclusion of scribal anomalies that may represent performance nuance or analytical guidance. In every case sufficient information is given that performers may make a "normalized" version if they so wish. The plainchant repertoire makes use of both medieval and modern sources.

As an acknowledgment of our lack of precise information about pre–Notre Dame rhythmic procedures, all earlier music, and that of Notre Dame monophony, is transcribed in noncommittal noteheads, with special signs for quilismas, liquescents, and plicas when needed. Barlines are used to indicate phrase divisions until the advent of the definitely metrical polyphony of late thirteenth-century France (ca. 1280).

The translations of Drs. Robert Crouse and Hans T. Runte aim at a close literal rendition of the original language, most often on an exact, line-by-line basis. Direct correlation has been given precedence over the greater literary elegance possible in paraphrase. In most cases the texts have been left to stand on their own, but occasionally, when the textual allusions are not readily apparent, brief commentary has been added.

Much help and assistance has made possible the completion of this anthology. The Research Development Fund of Dalhousie University has provided grants toward travel and the purchase of microfilms. The librarians of many European libraries have been helpful during personal visits or subsequently in the supplying of microfilms. The collaboration of my two translators, Drs. Robert Crouse and Hans T. Runte, has been greatly appreciated. A great pleasure has been the cooperation of Paul Hillier and both the Hilliard Ensemble and the Western Wind for their superb recordings of portions of the Anthology, and to Clifford Bartlett for his able coordination of that project. My wife, Barbara, has been the source of inspiration throughout, and to her I owe a very special word of thanks.

PART 1

Plainchant

Example 1.

Gradual *Viderunt omnes*

Montpellier, Fac. de med. H 159, fol. 94.

In this and subsequent plainchant transcriptions neumes are indicated by means of slurs and all notes are given as black noteheads except for the quilisma (⚹) and the liquescent (o). Diamond-shaped notes indicate tones notated as microtonally sharp in the manuscript *Mo H 159*.

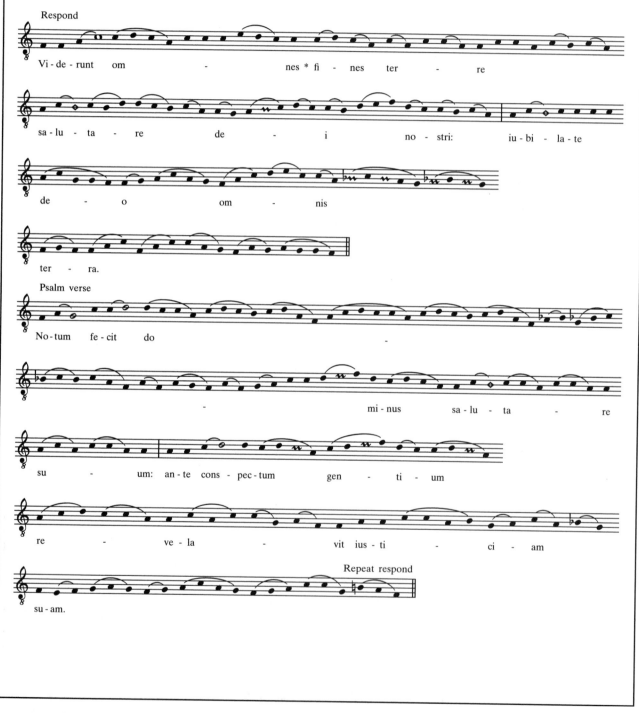

Example 1. Gradual *Viderunt omnes*

Respond

All the ends of the earth have seen the salvation of our God:
Rejoice in the Lord, all the earth.

Verse

The Lord hath made known his salvation:
His justice hath he revealed in the sight of the nations.

Respond

All the ends of the earth have seen the salvation of our God:
Rejoice in the Lord, all the earth.

Example 2.

Introit *Resurrexi*

Paris, B. N., lat. 1118 and 1871.

A. Complete chant

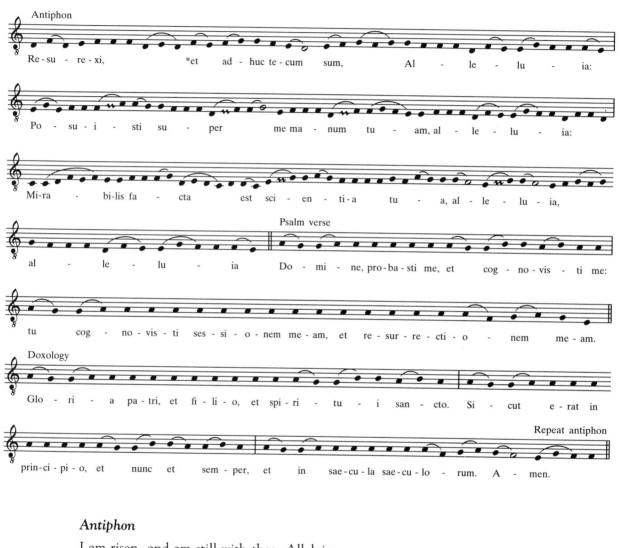

Antiphon
Re - su - re - xi, *et ad - huc te - cum sum, Al - le - lu - ia:

Po - su - i - sti su - per me ma - num tu - am, al - le - lu - ia:

Mi - ra - bi - lis fa - cta est sci - en - ti - a tu - a, al - le - lu - ia,

Psalm verse
al - le - lu - ia Do - mi - ne, pro - ba - sti me, et cog - no - vis - ti me:

tu cog - no - vis - ti ses - si - o - nem me - am, et re - sur - re - cti - o - nem me - am.

Doxology
Glo - ri - a pa - tri, et fi - li - o, et spi - ri - tu - i san - cto. Si - cut e - rat in

Repeat antiphon
prin - ci - pi - o, et nunc et sem - per, et in sae - cu - la sae - cu - lo - rum. A - men.

Antiphon

I am risen, and am still with thee, Alleluia:
Thou hast laid thine hand upon me, Alleluia:
Wonderful has become thy knowledge, Alleluia, Alleluia.

Verse

O Lord, thou hast searched me out, and known me:
Thou hast known my down sitting and my rising up.

Example 2. Introit *Resurrexi*

Doxology

Glory be to the Father, and to the Son, and to the Holy Spirit.
As it was in the beginning, is now, and ever shall be, and unto the ages of ages.
Amen.

Antiphon

I am risen, and am still with thee, Alleluia:
Thou hast laid thine hand upon me, Alleluia:
Wonderful has become thy knowledge, Alleluia, Alleluia.

The antiphon may also be repeated between the verse and Doxology.

B. Melodic trope of antiphon

C. Textual-melodic trope of antiphon

Examples 2b and 2c: Nicole Sevestre, "The Aquitanian Tropes of the Easter Introit: A Musical Analysis," *Journal of the Plainsong & Mediaeval Music Society* 3 (1980): 34–36; reprinted by permission of the Plainsong & Mediaeval Music Society.

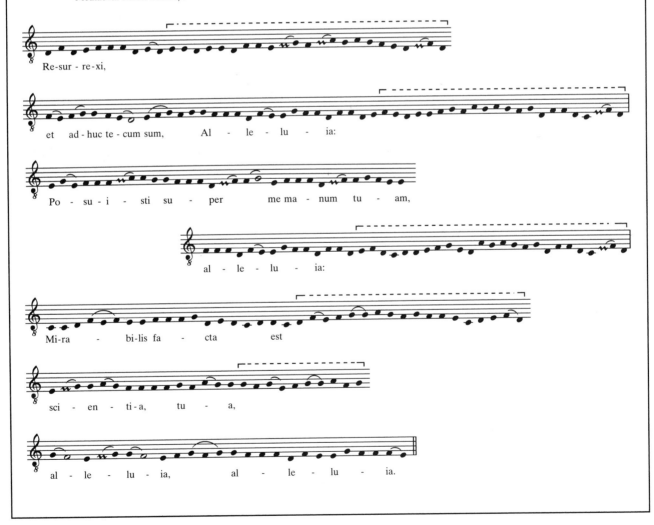

Example 2. Introit *Resurrexi*

I am risen and am still with thee, Alleluia:
Thou hast laid thine hand upon me, Alleluia:
Wonderful has become thy knowledge, Alleluia, Alleluia.

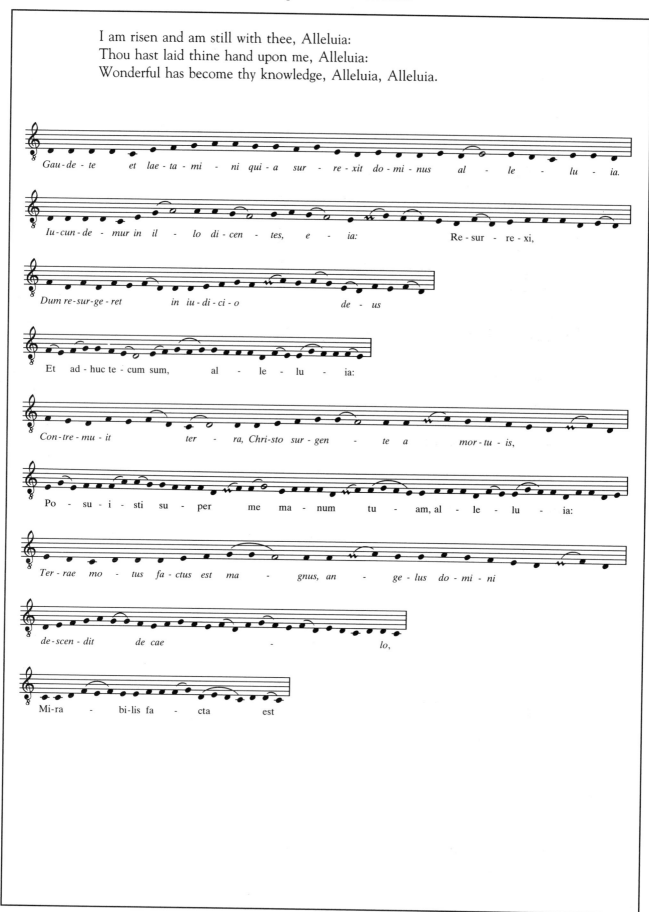

6

Example 2. Introit *Resurrexi*

Cu - sto - des   ve-lut mor - tu - i   ef - fec - ti   sunt

Sci - en - ti-a   tu - a,

Ni-mi - o   ti - mo - re an - gel - li,

Al - le - lu - ia,   al - le - lu - ia.

Rejoice and be glad, because the Lord is risen, Alleluia.
Let us rejoice in him, saying, Eia, Alleluia.
I am risen,
When God arose in judgment
And am still with thee, alleluia:
The earth trembled, when Christ arose from the dead,
Thou hast laid thy hand upon me, alleluia:
There was made a great earthquake,
   the angel of the Lord descended from heaven,
Wonderful has become
The guards became as dead men
Thy knowledge
For great fear of the angels,
Alleluia, alleluia.

Example 3.
Communion antiphon *Surrexit Dominus*

Montpellier, Fac. de med. H 159, fol. 41.

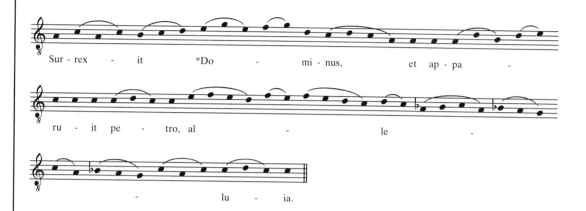

Sur - rex - it *Do - mi - nus, et ap - pa - ru - it pe - tro, al - le - - lu - ia.

The Lord is risen,
  and hath appeared unto Peter,
  Alleluia.

Example 4.
Alleluia: Angelus domini; Respondens

Montpellier, Fac. de med. H 159, fol. 67.

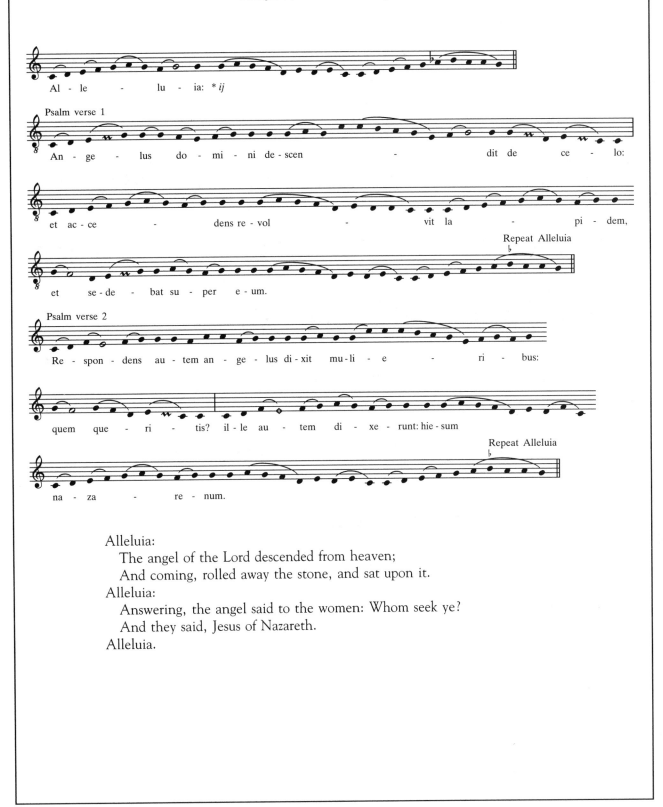

Al - le - lu - ia: * *ij*

Psalm verse 1

An - ge - lus do - mi - ni de - scen - dit de ce - lo:

et ac - ce - dens re - vol - vit la - pi - dem,

Repeat Alleluia

et se - de - bat su - per e - um.

Psalm verse 2

Re - spon - dens au - tem an - ge - lus di - xit mu - li - e - ri - bus:

quem que - ri - tis? il - le au - tem di - xe - runt: hie - sum

Repeat Alleluia

na - za - re - num.

Alleluia:
    The angel of the Lord descended from heaven;
    And coming, rolled away the stone, and sat upon it.
Alleluia:
    Answering, the angel said to the women: Whom seek ye?
    And they said, Jesus of Nazareth.
Alleluia.

Example 5.

Alleluia: Adorabo ad templum

London, B. L., Add. 12194, fol. 89.

Al - le - lu - ia. *ij

Psalm verse

Ad - o - ra - bo ad tem - plum

san - ctum tu - um: et con - fi -

te -

-

bor no - mi - ni tu - o.

Repeat Alleluia

Alleluia:
   I will worship towards thy holy temple:
   And I will confess thy name.
Alleluia.

Example 6.

Offertory *Stetit angelus*

A. Complete chant

Montpellier, Fac. de med. H 159, fol. 109'.

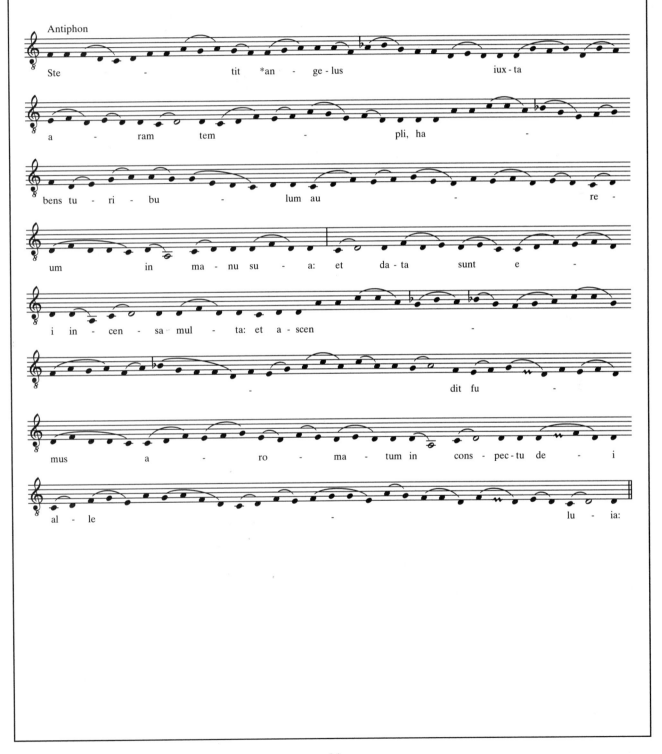

11

Example 6. Offertory *Stetit angelus*

Antiphon

An angel stood by the altar of the temple,
    having a golden censer in his hand:
And there was given unto him much incense:
    and the aromatic smoke ascended in the sight of the Lord,
Alleluia.

Verse

In the sight of the angels, I will sing to thee, O Lord:
And I will worship towards thy holy temple,
    and confess to thee, O Lord.

Antiphon

An angel stood by the altar of the temple,
    having a golden censer in his hand:
And there was given unto him much incense:
    and the aromatic smoke ascended in the sight of the Lord,
Alleluia.

Example 6. Offertory *Stetit angelus*

B. Prosula *Stetit Michael*

Paris lat. 1338

Gunilla Björkvall and Ruth Steiner, "Some Prosulas for Offertory Antiphons," *Journal of the Plainsong & Mediaeval Music Society* 5 (1982): 17, 19; reprinted by permission of the Plainsong & Mediaeval Music Society.

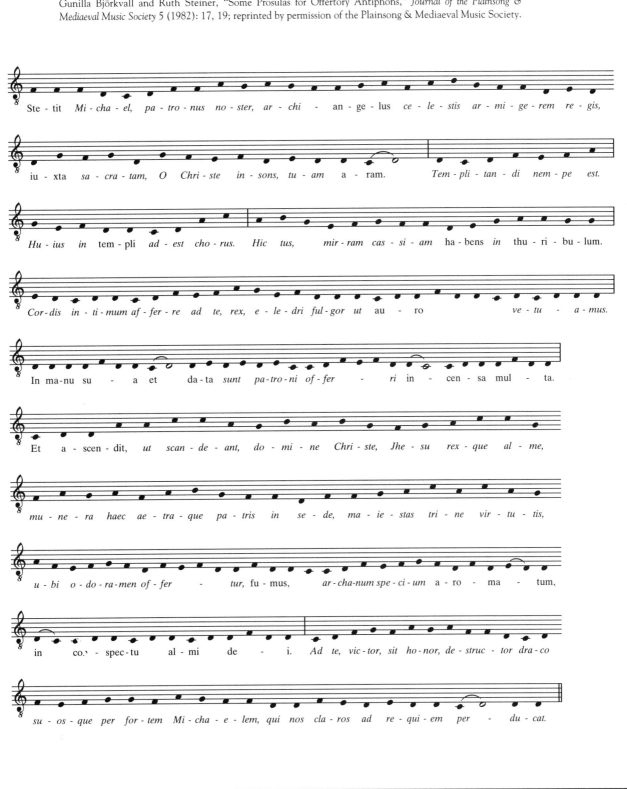

Ste - tit Mi - cha - el, pa - tro - nus no - ster, ar - chi - an - ge - lus ce - le - stis ar - mi - ge - rem re - gis,

iu - xta sa - cra - tam, O Chri - ste in - sons, tu - am a - ram. *Tem - pli - tan - di nem - pe est.*

Hu - ius in tem - pli ad - est cho - rus. Hic tus, mir - ram cas - si - am ha - bens in thu - ri - bu - lum.

Cor - dis in - ti - mum af - fer - re ad te, rex, e - le - dri ful - gor ut au - ro ve - tu - a - mus.

In ma - nu su - a et da - ta *sunt pa - tro - ni of - fer - ri in - cen - sa mul - ta.*

Et a - scen - dit, *ut scan - de - ant, do - mi - ne Chri - ste, Jhe - su rex - que al - me,*

mu - ne - ra haec ae - tra - que pa - tris in se - de, ma - ie - stas tri - ne vir - tu - tis,

u - bi o - do - ra - men of - fer - tur, fu - mus, *ar - cha - num spe - ci - um a - ro - ma - tum,*

in co - spec - tu al - mi de - i. *Ad te, vic - tor, sit ho - nor, de - struc - tor dra - co*

su - os - que per for - tem Mi - cha - e - lem, qui nos cla - ros ad re - qui - em per - du - cat.

Example 6. Offertory *Stetit angelus*

Michael stood, *our patron,* Archangel, *armor bearer of the heavenly King,*
By *thy consecrated* altar, *O guiltless Christ.*
The time of offering is at hand.
His choir is present in the temple.
He has *incense, myrrh, and cassia in the* censer.
We have been unwilling to offer up to thee the inner heart, O King,
     splendor, as with the gold of amber,
In the hand *of our patron also* was given much incense *to be offered.*
And it ascended, *that these gifts might also rise, O Lord Christ, Jesu,*
     King and bountiful, to the heavenly throne of Father, the
     majesty of triune power, where the perfume is offered, the smoke,
     of secret species of spices, in the sight of the bountiful God.
To thee, O Victor, be honor, destroyer of the dragon through strong
     Michael and his forces, who would lead us, glorious, to rest.

Example 7.
Great Responsory *Aspiciens a longe*

Salisbury, Cathedral Library, ms. 152, fol. 7′

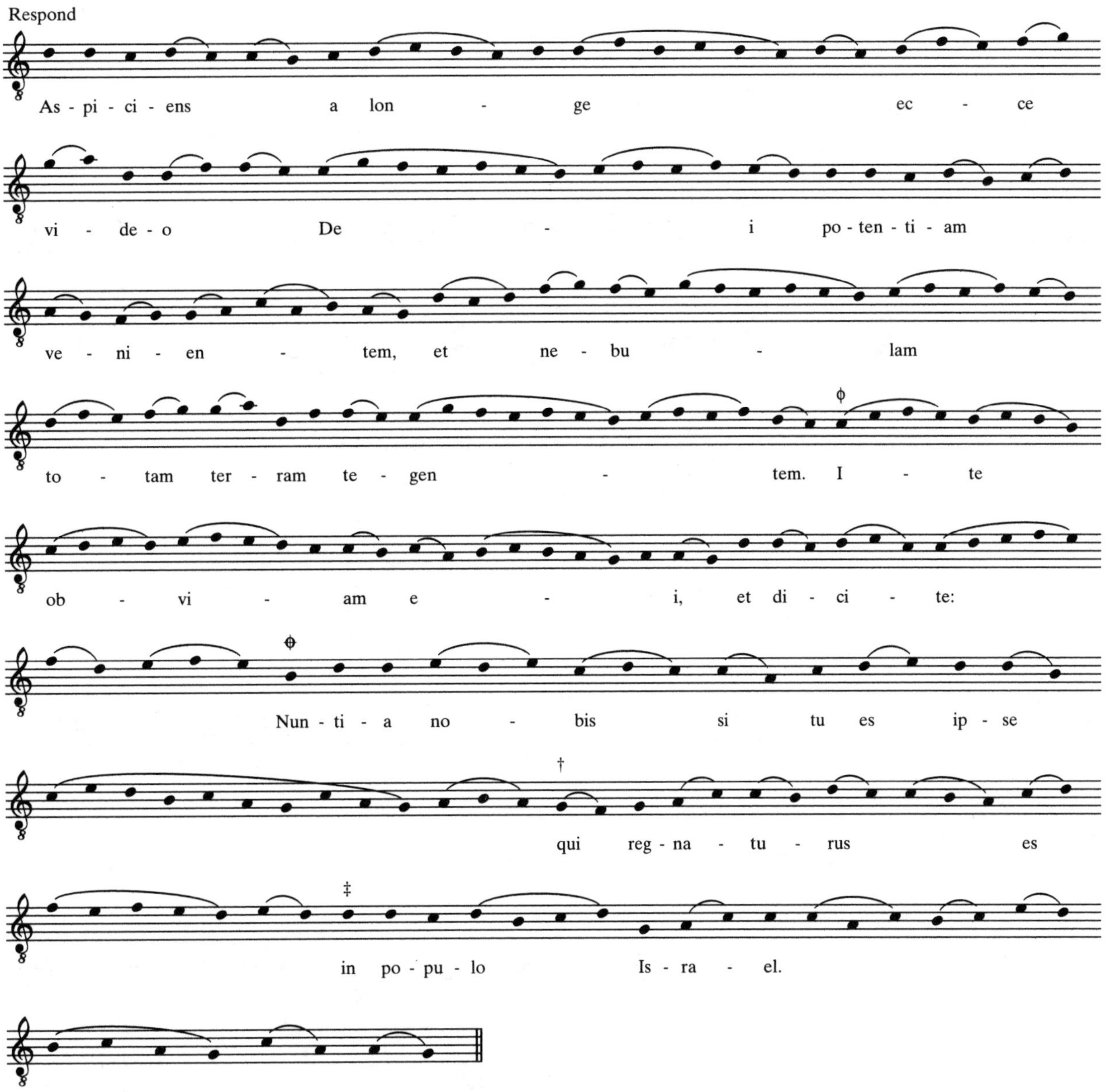

Respond

As - pi - ci - ens   a   lon -   ge   ec -   ce

vi - de - o   De -   i   po - ten - ti - am

ve - ni - en - tem, et   ne - bu -   lam

to - tam ter - ram te - gen -   tem. I - te

ob - vi - am   e -   i, et di - ci - te:

Nun - ti - a   no -   bis   si   tu   es   ip - se

qui   reg - na - tu - rus   es

in po - pu - lo   Is - ra - el.

15

Example 7. Great Responsory *Aspiciens a longe*

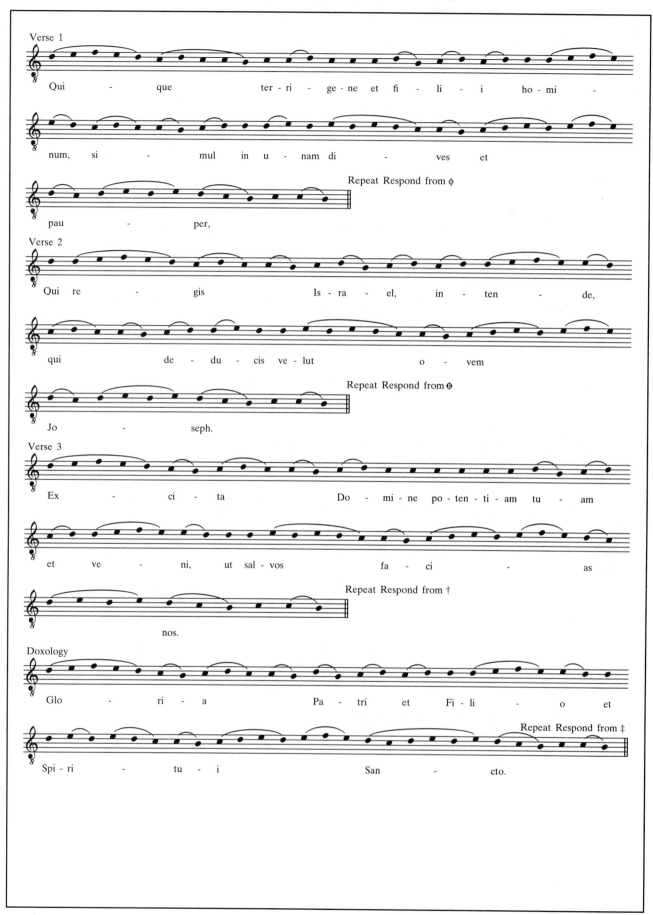

Example 7. Great Responsory *Aspiciens a longe*

Respond

Gazing from afar, behold I see
The power of God coming, and a cloud
Covering the whole earth.
Go ye forth to meet him, and say:
Tell us if thou art he
That will reign
Over the people Israel.

Verse 1

All ye of earth and sons of men,
Rich and poor together,

Repetendum

Go ye forth to meet him, and say:
Tell us if thou art he
That will reign
Over the people Israel.

Verse 2

Thou that rulest Israel, hear,
Thou that leadest Joseph like a sheep.

Repetendum

Tell us if thou art he
That will reign
Over the people Israel.

Verse 3

Raise up Thy power O Lord, and
Come to save us.

Repetendum

That will reign
Over the people Israel.

Doxology

Glory be to the Father and to the Son
and to the Holy Spirit,

Repetendum

Over the people Israel.

Example 8.

Tract *Vinea facta est*

Graduale Romanum, 188–89. © Abbaye Saint Pierre de Solesmes, France, 1974; used with permission.

The indications G_{1a}, F_a, etc., are for analytical purposes only.

Verse 1
G1a

Vi - ne - a   fa - cta est

Fa

di - le - cto

G2

in cor - nu,   in   lo - co u - be - ri.

Verse 2
G1b

Et ma - ce - ri - am cir-cum-de - dit, et cir-cum-fo - dit:

Fb

et plan - ta - vit vi - ne-am So - rec:

G2

et ae - di - fi - ca - vit tur - rim in me - di - o   e - jus.

Verse 3
Fb

Et tor - cu - lar fo - dit in e - a

G2

vi - ne - a   e - nim Do - mi - ni Sa - ba - oth,

G3b

do - mus Is - ra - el est.

18

Example 8. Tract *Vinea facta est*

My beloved made a vineyard,
Upon a hill, in a fruitful place.
And he fenced it and cultivated it:
And he planted it with choicest vines:
And he built a tower in the midst of it,
For the vineyard of the Lord is the house of Israel.

Example 9.

Tract *Laudate Dominum*

Graduale Romanum, 188–89. © Abbaye Saint Pierre de Solesmes, France, 1974; used with permission.

The indications G_{1a}, F_a, etc., are for analytical purposes only.

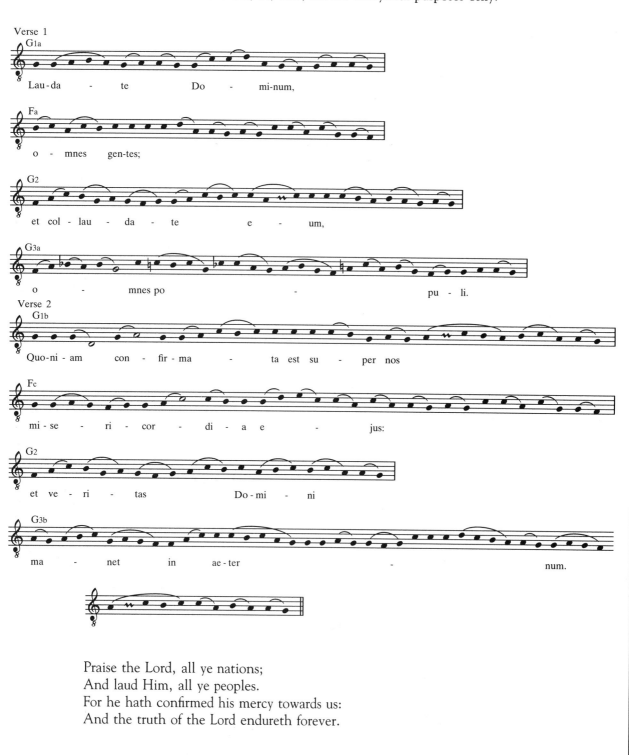

Praise the Lord, all ye nations;
And laud Him, all ye peoples.
For he hath confirmed his mercy towards us:
And the truth of the Lord endureth forever.

Example 10.

Kyrie Clemens Rector

A. Version of the modern *Graduale Romanum*

Graduale Romanum, 785–86. © Abbaye Saint Pierre de Solesmes, France 1974; used with permission.

1. Ky - ri - e e - le - i - son.
2. Ky - ri - e e - le - i - son.
3. Ky - ri - e e - le - i - son.
4. Chris - ste e - le - i - son.
5. Chris - ste e - le - i - son.
6. Chris - ste e - le - i - son.
7. Ky - ri - e e - le - i - son.
8. Ky - ri - e e - le - i - son.
9. Ky - ri - e e - le - i - son.

21

Example 10. Kyrie *Clemens Rector*

Lord have mercy upon us.
Christ have mercy upon us.
Lord have mercy upon us.

B. Texted version from the twelfth century

Paris, B. N. lat. 1235, f. 188

From Nancy van Deusen, *Music at Nevers Cathedral*; Musicological Studies 30 (Henryville, Pa.: Institute of Mediaeval Music, 1980), reprinted with permission.

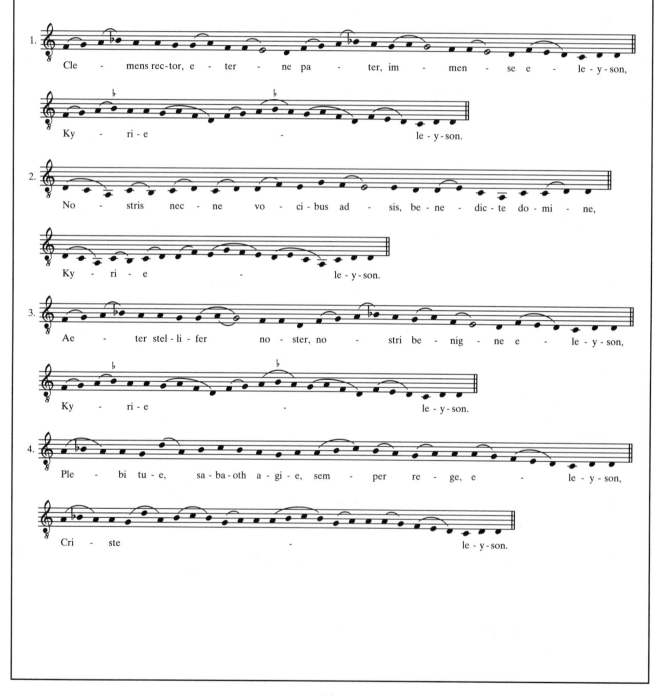

Example 10. Kyrie *Clemens Rector*

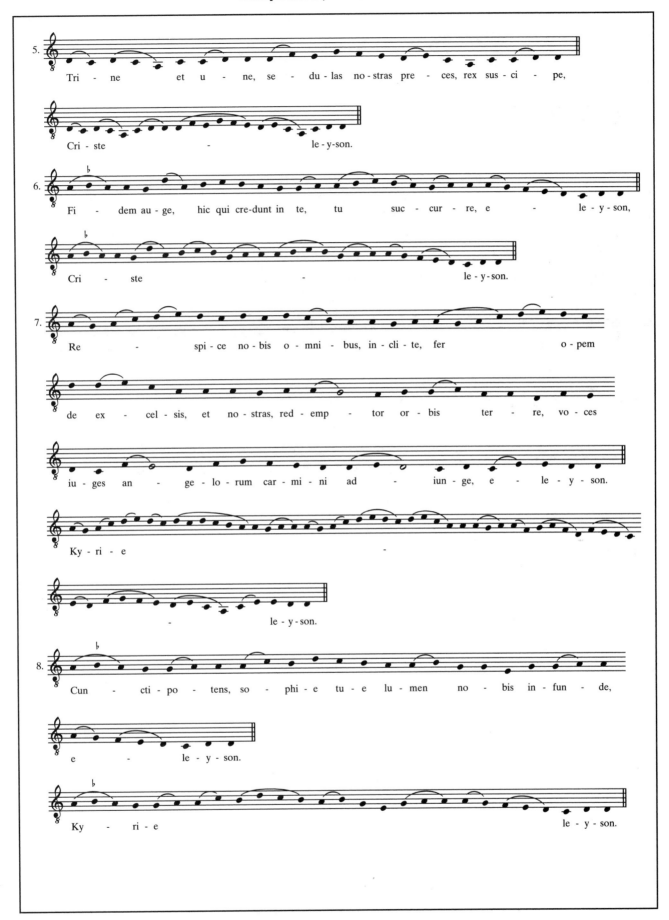

23

Example 10. Kyrie *Clemens Rector*

Example 10. *Kyrie Clemens Rector*

1. Kindly ruler, Father, eternal, boundless, have mercy upon us.
   Lord have mercy upon us.
2. And be attentive to our cries, blessed Lord.
   Lord have mercy upon us.
3. Our high star bearer, kind to us, have mercy upon us.
   Lord have mercy upon us.
4. Holy one of Sabaoth, ruler ever of thy people, have mercy upon us.
   Christ have mercy upon us.
5. Three in one, O King, our ardent prayers receive.
   Christ have mercy upon us.
6. Increase the faith, succor him who believes in Thee, have mercy upon us.
   Christ have mercy upon us.
7. Have respect unto us all, incline, bring aid from on high, and, Redeemer
   of the sphere of earth, join our joined voices to the song of the
   angels, have mercy upon us.
   Lord have mercy upon us.
8. Almighty, bestow upon us the light of thy wisdom, have mercy upon us.
   Lord have mercy upon us.
9. Three and one Lord, Lord,
   Who remainest in eternity with the Father,
   Thee with mouth and heart and mind,
   We sing now to Thee, O kind, good Jesu, we all beseech thee
   fervently, have mercy upon us.
   Have mercy upon us.

Example 11.

Agnus Dei *Redemptor mundi*

A. Version of the modern *Graduale Romanum*

Graduale Romanum, 718. © Abbaye Saint Pierre de Solesmes, France, 1974; used with permission.

O Lamb of God, that takest away the sins of the world,
    have mercy upon us;
O Lamb of God, that takest away the sins of the world,
    have mercy upon us;
O Lamb of God, that takest away the sins of the world,
    grant us peace.

Example 11. Agnus Dei *Redemptor mundi*

B. Troped version from the eleventh century

Paris, lat. 1121, fol. 4'

Paul Evans, *Early Trope Repertory* (Princeton, N.J.: Princeton University Press, 1970), 135–36; used by permission of Phot. Bibl. Nat. Paris.

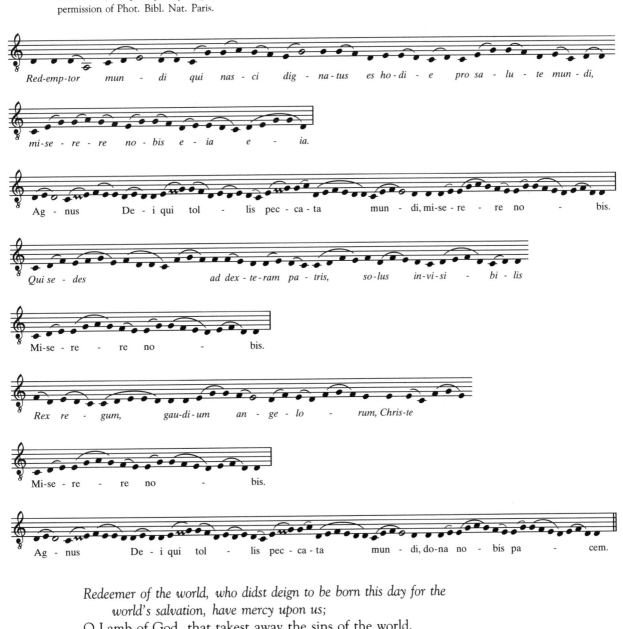

Red-emp-tor mun - di qui nas - ci dig - na - tus es ho-di - e pro sa - lu - te mun - di,

mi-se - re - re no - bis e - ia e - ia.

Ag - nus De - i qui tol - lis pec - ca - ta mun - di, mi-se - re - re no - bis.

Qui se - des ad dex - te - ram pa - tris, so-lus in - vi - si - bi - lis

Mi-se - re - re no - bis.

Rex re - gum, gau-di - um an - ge - lo - rum, Chris-te

Mi-se - re - re no - bis.

Ag - nus De - i qui tol - lis pec - ca - ta mun - di, do-na no - bis pa - cem.

Redeemer of the world, who didst deign to be born this day for the
    world's salvation, have mercy upon us;
O Lamb of God, that takest away the sins of the world,
    have mercy upon us;
Who sittest at the right hand of the Father, alone invisible,
    have mercy upon us;
King of kings, joy of the angels, Christ,
    have mercy upon us;
O Lamb of God, that takest away the sins of the world,
    grant us peace.

Example 12.

Sanctus III

Graduale Romanum, 723–24. © Abbaye Saint Pierre de Solesmes, France, 1974; used with permission.

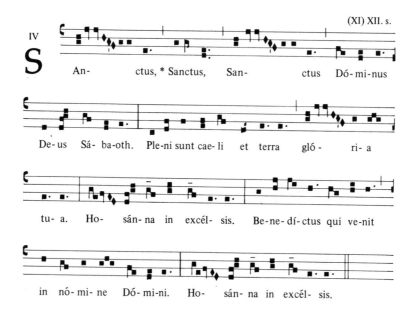

Holy, holy, holy, Lord God of Hosts.
Heaven and earth are full of thy glory.
Hosanna in the highest.
Blessed is he that cometh in the name of the Lord.
Hosanna in the highest.

Example 13.

Gloria IV

Graduale Romanum, 725–26. © Abbaye Saint Pierre de Solesmes, France, 1974; used with permission.

Example 13. Gloria IV

Dó- mi- ne De-us, Agnus De-i, Fí- li-us Pa- tris. Qui

tol-lis peccá- ta mundi, mi-se-ré- re no- bis. Qui tol- lis pec-

cá- ta mundi, súsci- pe depre- ca-ti- ónem nostram. Qui se-

des ad déx- te-ram Patris, mi-se- ré- re no- bis. Quó-ni- am

tu so-lus sanctus. Tu so-lus Dó- mi-nus. Tu so-lus Al-tís- si

mus, Ie- su Chri- ste. Cum San- cto Spí- ri- tu

in gló-ri- a De- i Pa- tris. A- men.

Glory be to God on high, and on earth peace to men of good will. We praise thee, we bless thee, we worship thee, we glorify thee, we give thanks to thee for thy great glory, O Lord God, heavenly King, God the Father Almighty.

O Lord, the only begotten Son, Jesus Christ; O Lord God, Lamb of God, Son of the Father, that takest away the sins of the world, have mercy upon us. Thou that takest away the sins of the world, receive our prayer. Thou that sittest at the right hand of God the Father, have mercy upon us.

For thou only art holy; thou only art the Lord; thou only, O Christ, with the Holy Spirit, art most high in the glory of God the Father.

Example 14.

Credo I

Graduale Romanum, 769–71. © Abbaye Saint Pierre de Solesmes, France, 1974; used with permission.

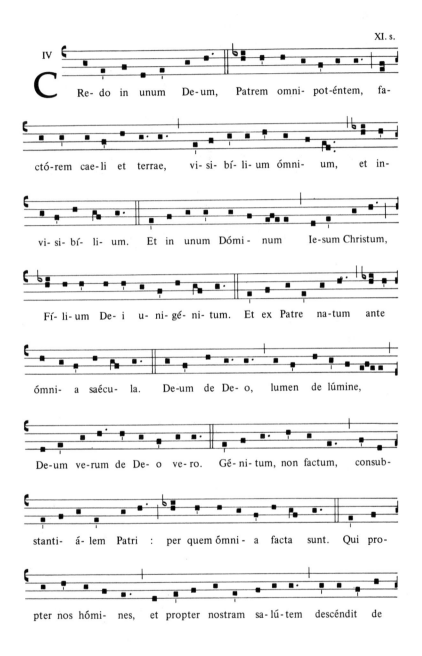

XI. s.

IV

C Re- do in unum De-um, Patrem omni- pot-éntem, fa-

ctó-rem cae-li et terrae, vi-si-bí-li-um ómni- um, et in-

vi-si-bí- li- um. Et in unum Dómi- num Ie-sum Christum,

Fí- li-um De- i u- ni-gé- ni-tum. Et ex Patre na-tum ante

ómni- a saécu- la. De-um de De- o, lumen de lúmine,

De-um ve-rum de De- o ve- ro. Gé- ni- tum, non factum, consub-

stanti- á- lem Patri : per quem ómni- a facta sunt. Qui pro-

pter nos hómi- nes, et propter nostram sa- lú-tem descéndit de

Example 14. Credo I

cae- lis. Et in-car- ná- tus est de Spí- ri- tu Sancto ex Ma- rí- a

Vir -gi- ne : Et homo factus est. Cru-ci- fí- xus ét- i- am pro

no- bis : sub Pónti- o Pi- lá- to passus, et sepúl- tus est. Et

re-surréxit tér- ti- a di- e, se- cúndum Scriptú-ras. Et ascén-

dit in caelum : se- det ad déxte - ram Patris. Et í- te- rum ven-

tú-rus est cum gló- ri- a, iu- di-cá- re vivos et mórtu- os :

cu- ius regni non e- rit fi- nis. Et in Spí- ri- tum Sanctum,

Dó- mi- num, et vi- vi- fi- cántem : qui ex Patre Fi- li- óque pro-

cé- dit. Qui cum Pa- tre et Fí- li- o simul ad- o- rá- tur, et

conglo- ri- fi- cá-tur : qui lo-cú-tus est per Prophé- tas. Et unam

Example 14. Credo I

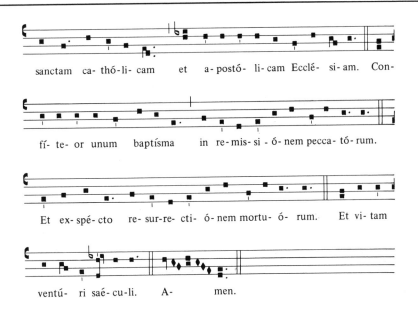

sanctam ca- thó- li- cam   et a- postó- li- cam Ecclé- si- am. Con-

fí- te- or unum baptísma in re- mis- si - ó- nem pecca- tó- rum.

Et ex- spé- cto re- sur- re- cti- ó- nem mortu- ó- rum. Et vi- tam

ventú- ri saé- cu- li.   A-   men.

I believe in one God, the Father almighty, Maker of heaven and earth, and of all things visible and invisible. And in one Lord, Jesus Christ, the only-begotten son of God. Born of the Father before all ages. God of God, light of light, true God of true God. Begotten, not made; of one being with the Father: by whom all things were made. Who for us men and for our salvation came down from heaven. And was made flesh by the Holy Spirit, of the Virgin Mary, and was made man. He also was crucified for us, suffered under Pontius Pilate, and was buried. And on the third day He arose again, according to the scriptures. And ascending into heaven, He sittest on the right hand of the Father. And he shall come again with glory to judge the living and the dead: and of His kingdom there shall be no end. And in the Holy Spirit, the Lord and Giver of Life, who proceedeth from the Father and the Son. Who together with the Father and Son is no less adored and glorified: who spoke by the prophets. And in one holy, universal, and apostolic Church. I confess one baptism for the remission of sins. And I look for the resurrection of the dead. And the life of the world to come. Amen.

Example 15.

Sequence *Regnantem sempiterna*

Reprinted from Richard Crocker, *The Early Medieval Sequence*, University of California Press. © 1977 the Regents of the University of California; used with permission.

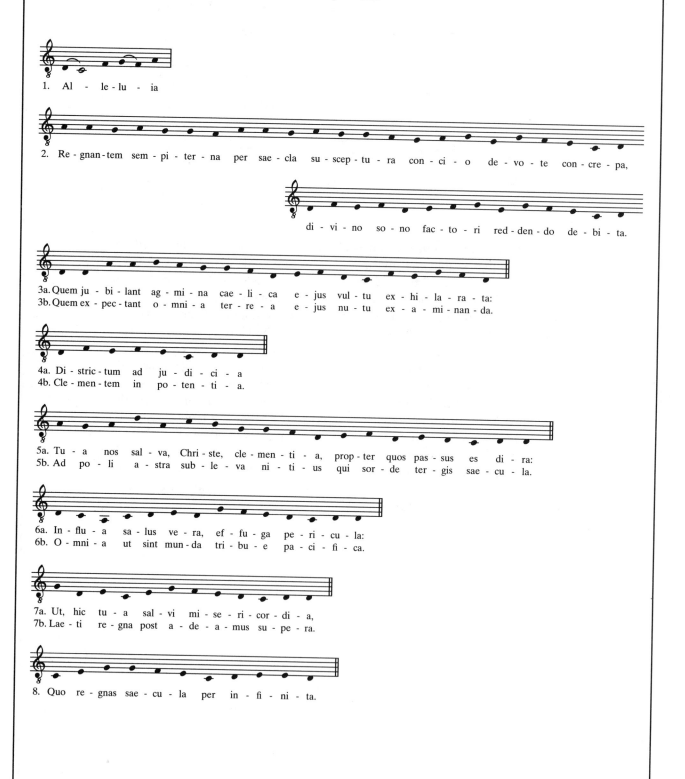

1. Al - le - lu - ia

2. Re - gnan - tem sem - pi - ter - na per sae - cla su - scep - tu - ra con - ci - o de - vo - te con - cre - pa,
di - vi - no so - no fac - to - ri red - den - do de - bi - ta.

3a. Quem ju - bi - lant ag - mi - na cae - li - ca e - jus vul - tu ex - hi - la - ra - ta:
3b. Quem ex - pec - tant o - mni - a ter - re - a e - jus nu - tu ex - a - mi - nan - da.

4a. Di - stric - tum ad ju - di - ci - a
4b. Cle - men - tem in po - ten - ti - a.

5a. Tu - a nos sal - va, Chri - ste, cle - men - ti - a, prop - ter quos pas - sus es di - ra:
5b. Ad po - li a - stra sub - le - va ni - ti - us qui sor - de ter - gis sae - cu - la.

6a. In - flu - a sa - lus ve - ra, ef - fu - ga pe - ri - cu - la:
6b. O - mni - a ut sint mun - da tri - bu - e pa - ci - fi - ca.

7a. Ut, hic tu - a sal - vi mi - se - ri - cor - di - a,
7b. Lae - ti re - gna post a - de - a - mus su - pe - ra.

8. Quo re - gnas sae - cu - la per in - fi - ni - ta.

34

Example 15. Sequence *Regnantem sempiterna*

1. Alleluia
2. O ye people, praise devoutly him who reigns forever through the ages yet to come, rendering with divine sound what is due to the creator.
3a. Whom the heavenly hosts celebrate, made joyful by his countenance:
3b. Whom all the lands await, to be judged by his will.
4a. Severe in judgments
4b. Merciful in power.
5a. Save us, O Christ, by thy mercy, for whom thou hast suffered dreadful things:
5b. Raise to the heights of heaven the shining ones, thou that makest the ages clear from stain.
6a. Bestow true salvation, dispel dangers:
6b. Grant all things, such as may be pure and peaceable,
7a. That there, saved by thy mercy,
7b. Joyful, we may go to the heavenly kingdom hereafter.
8. Wherein thou dost reign through endless ages.

PART 2

Early Organum

Example 16.

Examples of Parallel Organum from the *Musica enchiriadis*

In Examples 16–26 the plainchant melody (*vox principalis*) is notated in white noteheads, the *vox organalis* in black noteheads, liquescents in small noteheads.

A. At the octave

Tu pa - tris sem - pi - ter - nus es fi - li - us

B. At the fifth

Tu pa - tris sem - pi - ter - nus es fi - li - us

C. At the fourth

Tu pa - tris sem - pi - ter - nus es fi - li - us

Example 16. Examples of Parallel Organum from the *Musica enchiriadis*

D. Composite parallel organum at the fifth

Sit glo - ri - a do - mi - ni in se - cu - la, le - ta - bi - tur do - mi - nus in

o - pe - ri - bus su - is.

A, B, and C.

Thou art the Son of the everlasting Father.

D.

Glory be to the Lord forever;
The Lord will rejoice in his works.

Example 17.

Examples of Oblique Organum

A. From the *Musica enchiriadis*

Rex coe - li Do - mi - ne ma - ris un - di - so - ni
Ti - ta - nis ni - ti - di squa - li - di - que so - li,

Te hu - mi - les fa - mu - li mo - du - lis ve - ne - ran - do pi - is
Se ju - be - as fla - gi - tant va - ri - is li - be - ra - re ma - lis.

B. From the first Bamberg dialogue

Scan - de ce - li tem - pla vir - go dig - na tan - to foe - de - re

C. From the first Bamberg dialogue

Te sa - cer sub - i - re cel - sa po - scit a - stra Jup - pi - ter

Example 17. Examples of Oblique Organum

D. From the second Bamberg dialogue

Gra - tu - le - tur o - mnis ca - ro na - to Chris - to do - mi - no

A.

King of heaven, Lord of the roaring sea,
And of the parched land of bright Titanus,
Thy humble servants, worshipping thee in pious measures,
Beseech thee to deliver them from varied evils.

B.

Scale the temple of heaven, O Virgin, worthy of so great a covenant.

C.

Thee the holy one beseeches, to ascend the lofty heaven of Jupiter.

D.

Let all rejoice in Christ the Lord born in the flesh.

Example 18.

Alleluia: Angelus domini; Respondens
(oblique organum)

Reconstructed by A. Holschneider, *Die Organa von Winchester* (Hildesheim: Georg Olms Verlag, 1968), 110; reprinted by permission.

For plainchant version, see Example 4.

Example 18. *Alleluia: Angelus domini; Respondens*

Alleluia:
    The angel of the Lord descended from heaven;
    And coming, rolled away the stone, and sat upon it.
Alleluia:
    Answering, the angel said to the women: "Whom seek ye?"
    And they said, "Jesus of Nazareth."
Alleluia.

PART 3

Free Organum

Example 19.

Cunctipotens genitor Deus (texted Kyrie)

Milan, Bib. Amb., M17.sup. (*Ad organum faciendum*)

Letter notation. Phrase marks follow those of the manuscript.

Cun - cti - po - tens ge - ni - tor De - us,   om - ni - cre - a - tor,   e   -   ley - son.

Chri - ste De - i   splen - dor,   vir - tus pa - tris - que   so - phi - a,   e   -   ley - son.

Am - bo - rum   sa - crum   spi - ra - men,   ne - xus   a - mor - que,   e   -   ley - son.

O God, Almighty Father, all creating, have mercy upon us.
O Christ, splendor, power and wisdom of the Father, have mercy upon us.
O sacred breath of both, and bond of love, have mercy upon us.

Example 20.

Alleluia: Justus ut palma

This version is a composite of the two main manuscripts of the *Ad organum faciendum*. The musical pitches are those of *BerA* (Berlin, Staatsbibliothek der Stiftung Preussischer Kulturbesitz, MS theol. lat. qu. 261), fol. 48′, while phrase indications are from Milan, Bib. Amb., M.17.sup, fol. 58.

Letter notation.

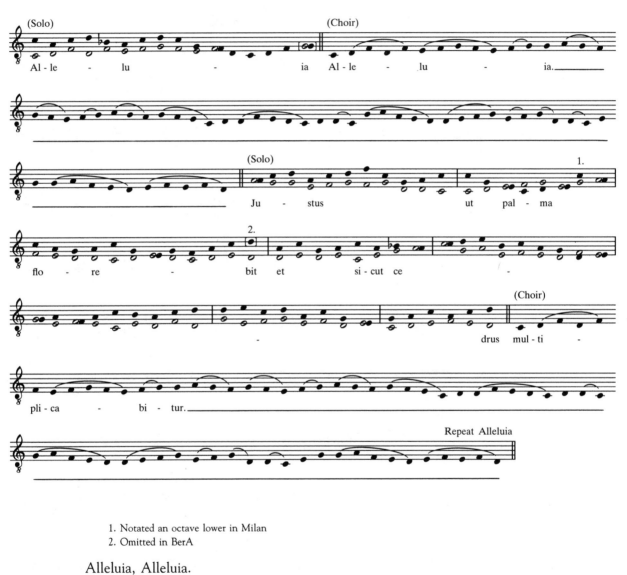

1. Notated an octave lower in Milan
2. Omitted in BerA

Alleluia, Alleluia.
    The just shall flourish as a palm tree:
    And spread abroad as a cedar.
Alleluia.

Example 21.

Alleluia: O quam pulchra est

Autun, Bibl. de la ville, Ms. 40 B, fol. 63.

Letter notation. The dots indicate neume divisions.

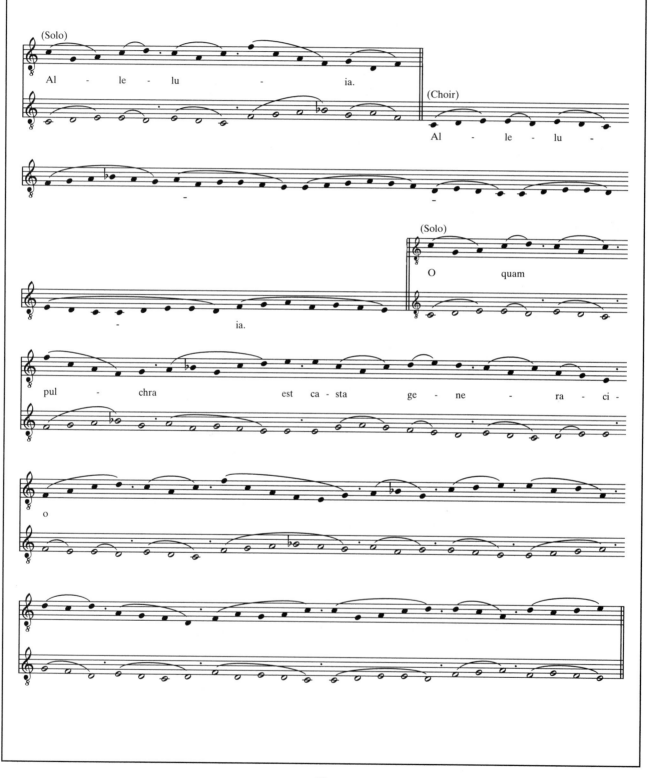

48

Example 21. *Alleluia: O quam pulchra est*

Alleluia.
   O how fair with brightness is the pure begetting.
Alleluia.

49

Example 22.

Ut tuo propitiatus (responsory verse)

Oxford, Bodleian Library, Bodley 572, fol. 49'.

Letter notation. The original contains a number of possibly extraneous marks and lines that are usually interpreted as additional (but often illogical) notes. These are bypassed in this transcription in favor of a strict note-against-note style. The dots of division seem more likely to indicate phrasing than neumes.

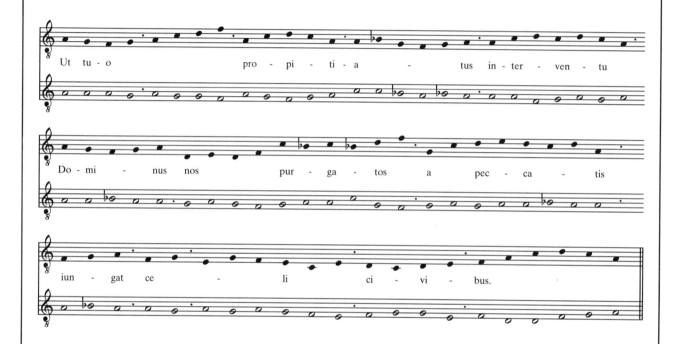

Ut tu - o pro - pi - ti - a - tus in - ter - ven - tu

Do - mi - nus nos pur - ga - tos a pec - ca - tis

iun - gat ce - li ci - vi - bus.

So that the Lord, moved by thine intercession, might join us, purged of sin, to the citizens of heaven.

Example 23.

Alleluia: Surrexit Christus

Chartres, Bibl. de la ville, Ms. 109, fol. 75.

This manuscript possibly originated in Chartres itself, but was destroyed during World War II. The present versions of Examples 23 and 24 are based on the facsimile and transcription published by H. M. Bannister in 1911 ("Un fragment inédit de 'discantus'," *Revue grégorienne* 1 [1911]: 29–33). The one-page fragment contains settings for the Easter season and is notated on a four-line dry-point staff.

Alleluia, Alleluia.
    Christ has risen, who created all things:
    And he was merciful to the human race.
Alleluia.

51

Example 24.

Alleluia: Angelus domini

Chartres 109, fol. 75.

For plainchant version, see Example 4.

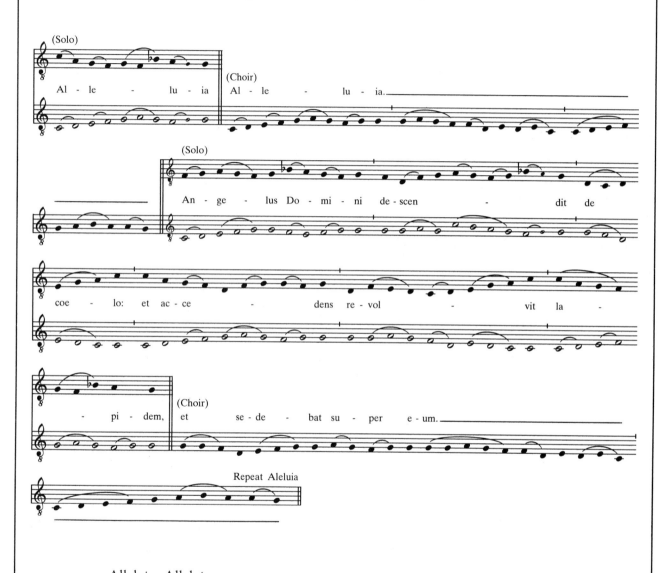

Alleluia, Alleluia.
The angel of the Lord descended from heaven:
And came, and rolled away the stone, and sat upon it.
Alleluia.

Example 25.

Dicant nunc Judei (processional antiphon verse)

Chartres 109, fol. 75; Oxford, Rawl. C. 892, fol. 67'.

Dicant nunc Judei is the verse of the processional antiphon *Christus resurgens* for the Easter season. The setting is incomplete in Chartres 109, but can be found in the late twelfth-century Irish manuscript Rawl. C. 892, where, however, page trimming has removed some of the conclusion of the organal voice.

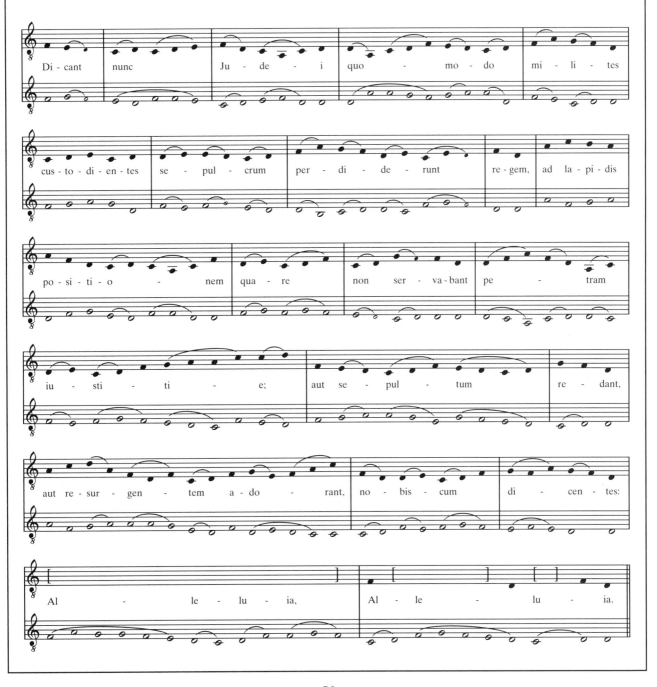

Example 25. *Dicant nunc Judei*

Let the Jews now say how the soldiers guarding the sepulchre lost the King at the placing of the stone, wherefore they did not keep the rock of righteousness; let them either produce the buried one, or let them adore with us the rising one, saying, Alleluia, Alleluia.

PART 4

Aquitanian Sacred Music

Example 26.

Congaudeat ecclesia (monophonic versus)

Paris, B. N., lat. 1139, fol. 51.

Con - gau - de - at ec - cle - si - a Per hec sa - cra sol - lemp - ni - a,

Et gau - det cum le - ti - ti - a Let - ti du - cat tri - pu - di - a

Er - go gau - de gau - di - o, Ju - ve - ni - lis con - ci - o, Ac de pa - tris fo - li - o

Vir - gi - nis in gre - mi - o Chri - sto De - i fi - li - o Na - to.

Refrain

No - va pu - er - pe - ri - o Fac - to Gau - de - at ho - mo, Gau - de - at ho - mo

Gau - de - at - ho - mo.

Let the church rejoice
In this holy festival
And let her rejoice with gladness.
Joyful, let her lead the dances.
   Therefore rejoice with joy
   O company of youth;
   For a leaf from the Father,
   In the womb of the Virgin,
   Christ the Son of God
   Is born.
In the newborn child
Let men rejoice,
Let men rejoice,
Let men rejoice.

56

Example 27.

Plebs domini (monophonic versus)

Paris, B. N., lat. 3549, fol. 167′.

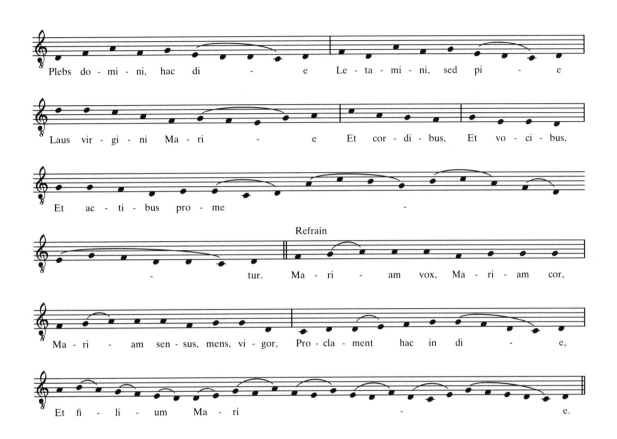

Plebs do - mi - ni, hac di - e Le - ta - mi - ni, sed pi - e

Laus vir - gi - ni Ma - ri - e Et cor - di - bus, Et vo - ci - bus,

Et ac - ti - bus pro - me -

Refrain

- tur. Ma - ri - am vox, Ma - ri - am cor,

Ma - ri - am sen - sus, mens, vi - gor, Pro - cla - ment hac in di - e,

Et fi - li - um Ma - ri - e.

1. People of the Lord, this day,
   Let us rejoice; but piously let
   Praise to the Virgin Mary,
   With hearts,
   And words,
   And deeds, be offered.

Refrain

Let voice, heart,
Sense, mind, and strength
Proclaim Mary on this day,
And the Son of Mary.

Example 27. *Plebs domini*

2. Homo Deus est natus,
   Homo reus renatus,
   Judaeus est caecatus,
      Rex parvulus,
      Vas figulus,
      Fons rivulus creatur.

   God is born a man,
   Guilty man reborn;
   The Jew is blind.
      The King is made a child,
      The pot is made the potter,
      The stream is made the spring.

3. Res agitur novella,
   Sol oritur de stella,
   Nec laeditur puella;
      Puella est,
      Quae mater est,
      Quod est, non est natura.

   A new thing is done;
   The sun arises from the star,
   Nor is the maiden spoiled;
      She is a maiden
      Who is a mother,
      What is, is not by nature.

4. Infans subest papillae,
   Sed Deus est et ille,
   Rex puer est ancillae,
      Rex aetheris,
      Sub pauperis,
      Mulieris est cura.

   The infant lies beneath the breasts,
   But he is also God.
   The king is child of the handmaiden.
      The king of heaven
      Is in the care
      Of a pauper woman.

5. Sol nuntius diei,
   Qui filius est Dei
   Et radius par ei,
      Quo tegitur,
      Deteditur,
      Fit igitur res mira.

   The sun, the messenger of day,
   Who is the Son of God,
   And a ray equal to him,
      By whom he is veiled
      He is revealed;
      A wonder thus is done.

6. Dum gratia subvenit,
   In propria rex venit,
   Opprobria invenit,
      Omnipotens
      Fit impotens,
      O pia mens, respira.

   When grace subvened
   The king came to his own.
   He found reproach.
      The almighty one
      Becomes powerless
      O pious mind, recover breath.

7. Hoc zabulus explorat,
   Hoc aemulus ignorat,
   Hoc angelus adorat,
      Hoc omnium
      Ingenium
      Non monimum miratur.

   This the devil discovers,
   This the envious one does not recognize,
   This the angel adores,
      This the nature of all things
      Not a little
      Wonders at.

8. Hoc sobrie decanta,
   Stirps gratiae, gens sancta,
   Materie de tanta
      Cum gaudio
      Fit mentio,
      Jam lectio legatur.

   This prudently repeat,
   Progeny of grace, holy race.
   Of the subject of such great things,
      With gladness
      Make mention.
      Now let the lesson be read.

Example 28.

Letabundi jubilemus (monophonic versus)

Paris, B. N., lat. 1139, fol. 58.

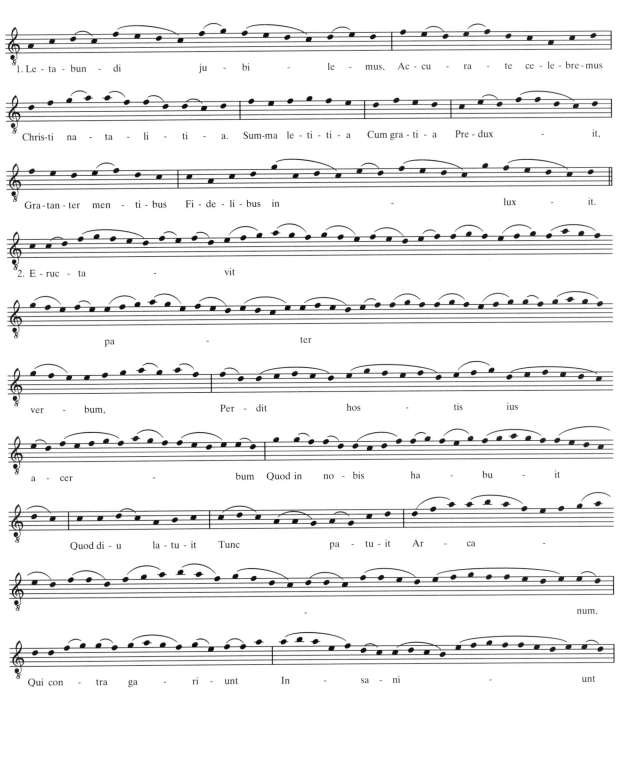

1. Le - ta - bun - di ju - bi - le - mus, Ac - cu - ra - te ce - le - bre - mus

Chris-ti na - ta - li - ti - a. Sum-ma le - ti - ti - a Cum gra - ti - a Pre - dux - it,

Gra - tan - ter men - ti - bus Fi - de - li - bus in - lux - it.

2. E - ruc - ta - vit

pa - ter

ver - bum, Per - dit hos - tis ius

a - cer - bum Quod in no - bis ha - bu - it

Quod di - u la - tu - it Tunc pa - tu - it Ar - ca -

num,

Qui con - tra ga - ri - unt In - sa - ni - unt

59

Example 28. *Letabundi jubilemus*

In ... va - ... num.

3. O - ra dig - na pre - di - ca - ri Cu - i non va - lent com - pa - ra - ri

Quan - ta - vis mi - ra - cu - la. Fe - rit vir - gin - cu - la Per se - cu - la

Rec - to - rem Con - cep - tum e - di - dit Nec per - di - dit

Pu - do - rem.

1. Let us rejoice with gladness.
   Let us celebrate attentively
   The Nativity of Christ.
   > Highest joyfulness
   > With grace
   > He has brought forth;
   > Joyfully has he enlightened
   > Faithful minds.

2. The Father has brought forth his Word.
   The enemy has lost the bitter right
   Which he had over us.
   > What long lay hidden
   > The mystery
   > Has revealed.
   > Those who babble against it
   > Rage in vain.

3. O matter worthy of proclamation,
   To which cannot be compared
   However great a miracle.
   > The little virgin bore
   > The ruler
   > Of the ages;
   > Conceived, she brought him forth,
   > Nor lost her maidenhood.

Example 29.

Novum festum celebremus

Due to their changed and now somewhat uncertain meaning in performance, the liquescent note, which begins to take on some of the attributes of the plica, is indicated by a small notehead in examples of pre–Notre Dame polyphony. The quilisma, which now seems to indicate a kind of stationary tremolo, is indicated by ⸱⸾⸱.

A. Monophonic versus

Paris, B. N., lat. 3549, fol. 165'.

No - vum fes - tum ce - le - bre - mus

No - vos can - tus et can - te - mus

Fac - ta re - rum no - vi - ta - te

In no - va sol - lem - ni - ta - te

61

Example 29. *Novum festum celebremus*

B. Polyphonic versus

Paris, B. N., lat. 1371, fol. 40'.

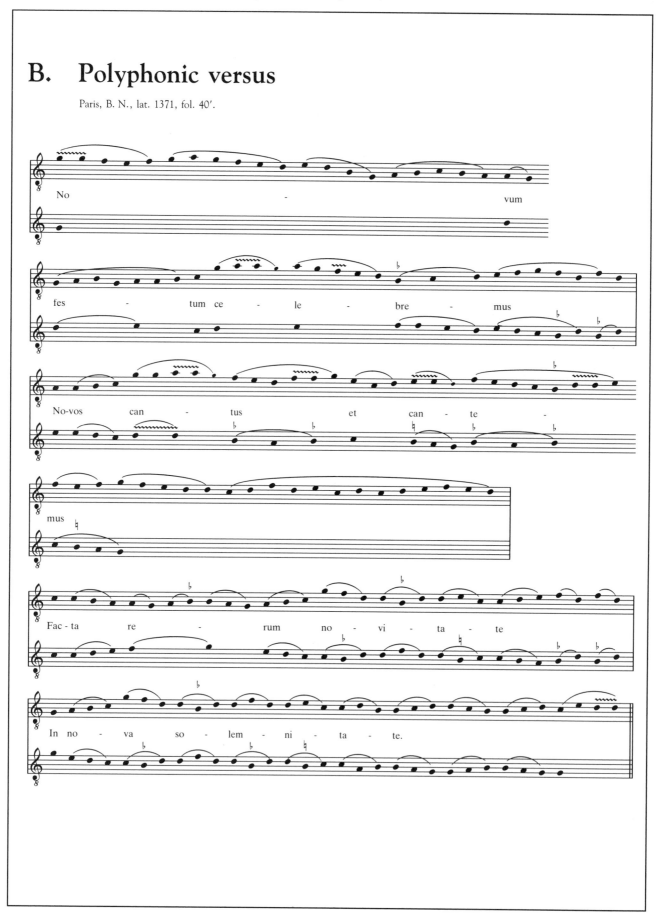

Example 29. *Novum festum celebremus*

1. Let us celebrate a new festival,
   And let us sing new songs,
   For the newness of the things established,
   In the new festivity.

2. Servus erat primus homo
   Factus pro comesto pomo
   Ob hoc penas est daturus
   Velit nolit moriturus

The first man was made a slave
On account of the eaten apple,
For which he would be given as punishment
That, willy-nilly, he would die.

3. Dolens ergo creaturam
   Mundi factor perituram
   Sola ductus pietate
   Sexta descendit aetate

The maker of the world, therefore grieving
That his creature would perish,
Led by compassion only,
In the sixth age descended.

4. Et assumens quod non erat
   Manens tamen hoc quod erat
   Est non-homo factus homo
   Deus ut salvetur homo

And taking what he was not,
Yet remaining what he was,
Not-man, God, was made man,
That man might be saved.

5. Venit ergo predicare
   Cunctis et salutem dare
   Regna dat aeternitatis
   Si desistant a peccatis

He came, therefore, to proclaim to all,
And to give salvation.
He gives the kingdom of eternity,
If they desist from sins.

6. Sed Maria Magdalena
   Peccatorum labe plena
   Ut audivit ejus verbum
   Rea crimen flet acerbum

But Mary Magdalene,
Stained, full of sins,
As she heard his word,
Bewailed her bitter crime.

7. Flendo sua rigat ora
   Jam non est in ulla mora
   Mundi linquens blandimenta
   Christum quaerens fert unguenta.

By weeping, she benumbs her mouth;
Now she makes no delay,
Forsaking the world's blandishments,
Seeking Christ, she bears ointments.

Example 30.

Orienti oriens (polyphonic versus)

Paris, B. N., lat. 3719, fol. 77.

O

Or - ri - en - ti o - ri - ens

Stel - la no - va cla - ru - it

Et Ja - cob e - gre - di - ens

Lu - ci - fer e - mi - cu - it

Ba - la - am pre - sa - gi - ens

Ut o - lim e - do - cu - it.

Example 30. *Orienti oriens*

1. O rising from the east
     A new star has shone;
   And Jacob departing,
     Lucifer has sprung forth,
   Balaam foreshadowing,
     As once he taught.

2. Auctor secli nascitur
     Seculorum vespere
   Ac magis agnoscitur
     Artifex in opere
   Adorandus creditur
     Unus trino munere

   The Author of the age is born
     In the evening of the ages;
   Yet better is known
     The Maker in the work.
   It is believed the One in Three
     Must be adored with tribute.

3. In ture divinitas
     In auro dominium
   In murra mortalitas
     Et carnis supplicium
   Et hec tria caritas
     Offerat fidelium.

   In incense, divinity;
     In gold, kingship;
   In myrrh, mortality,
     And suffering of the flesh.
   And the charity of the faithful
     Offers these three.

Example 31.

Lux refulget (polyphonic versus)

London, B. L., add. 36881, fol. 8'.

Example 31. *Lux refulget*

nu - el Cu - ius no - men cla - ru - it in Is - ra -
- el.

Light sent from heaven shines.
Here is the day foretold by the prophets.
Let the church rejoice,
Resounding with glorious songs of praise,
By voices with harmony
Resounding the great birthday:
Emmanuel, Emmanuel,
Whose name is great in Israel.

Example 32.

Nuptialis hodie (polyphonic versus)

Paris, B. N., lat. 3549, fol. 153′.

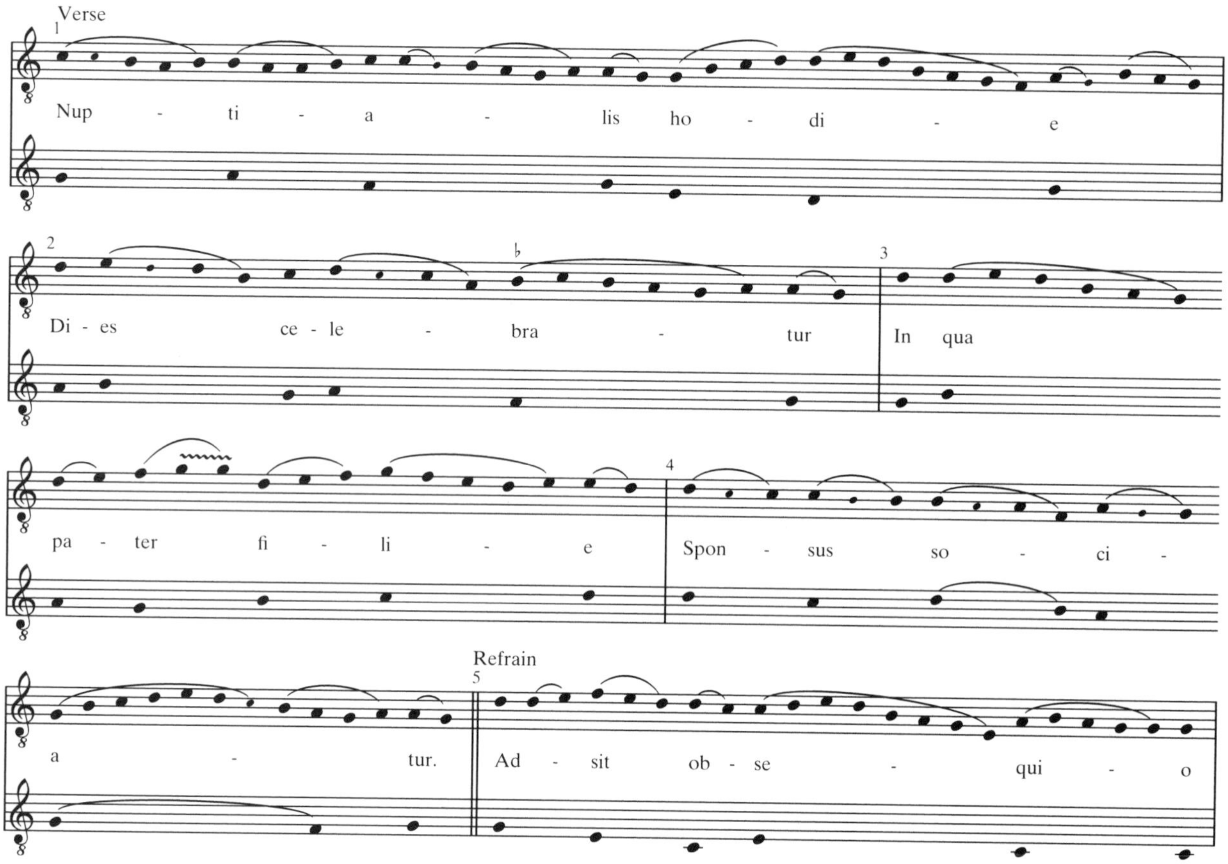

Verse

Nup - ti - a - lis ho - di - e

Di - es ce - le - bra - tur In qua

pa - ter fi - li - e Spon - sus so - ci -

Refrain

a - tur. Ad - sit ob - se - qui - o

Example 32. *Nuptialis hodie*

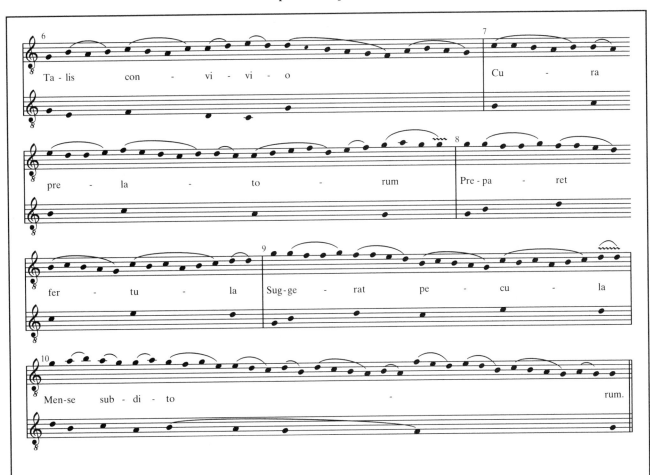

Ta - lis con - vi - vi - o Cu - ra

pre - la - to - rum Pre - pa - ret

fer - tu - la Sug - ge - rat pe - cu - la

Men-se sub - di - to rum.

Verse 1

The day of the wedding
Today is celebrated,
In which the Father to the daughter
As bridegroom is united.

Refrain

Let indulgence be present.
Take care for such
A banquet of offerings:
Prepare the cakes
Bring on the meats,
For furnishing the table.

Verse 2

Singularis igitur   One by one therefore,
Jessea mandata;   The Jessean commands;
Sed quaterni sequitur   But four by four follows
Increscente vita.   With increasing life.

Example 33.

Preconia virginis laudum (respond prose)

Paris, B. N., lat. 3719, fol. 48.

1a. Pre - co - ni - a vir-gi - nis lau -
1b. Que ge - nu - it do-mi - num re -

dum cla - ra - que can - ti - ca
gem re - gen - tem o - mni - a

2a. Po - sci - mus do - mi - na

Sol - ve mi-se - ro - rum vin-cu - la

2b. Tor - ge no - stra fa - ci

no - ra Ab-lu - en - do de-lic - ta

Example 33. *Preconia virginis laudum*

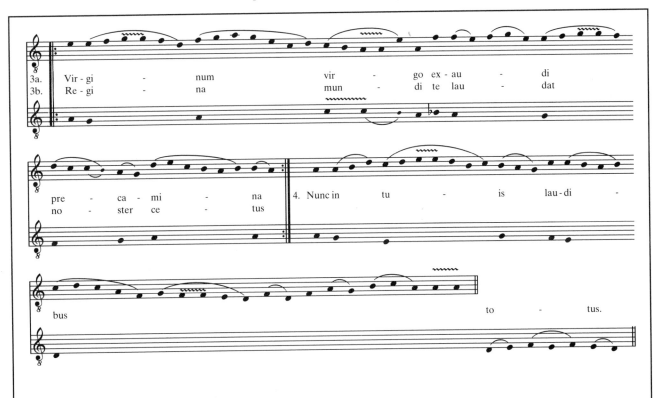

1a. Songs of praise, and great songs of praises of the virgin
1b. Who begot the Lord, the King, ruling all things.
2a. We beseech thee, Lady, loose the chains of misery,
2b. Wipe clean our crimes by washing away transgressions.
3a. Virgin of virgins, hear our supplications;
3b. Queen of the world, our company praises thee.
4. Now in thy praises wholly.

PART 5

Aquitanian Secular Music

Example 34.

Bernart de Ventadorn (second half, twelfth century), *La dousa votz* (two transmissions)

a. Paris, B. N., f. frç. 22543 (Chansonnier d'Urfe), fol. 57c (ca. 1300).
b. Paris, B. N., f. frç. 20050 (Chansonnier de St. Germain des Prés), fol. 86 (mid-fourteenth century).

1. The sweet voice I've heard
   Of the wild nightingale,
   And into my heart it has leaped,
   So that all the worry
   And the bad troubles that love gives me
   It has soothed and softened.
   And well could I use
   Another's joy in my distress.

Example 34. Bernart de Ventadorn, *La dousa votz*

2. Ben es totz om d'avol vida
   C'ab joi non a son estatge
   E qui vas amor no guida
   So cor e so dezirer;
   Car tot can es s'abandona
   Vas joi e refrim' e sona:
   Prat e deves e verger,
   Landes e pla e boschatge.

Indeed, any man is of vile life
Who with joy does not have his estate,
And who toward love does not guide
His heart and his desire;
For everything that is abandons itself
To joy and rings and resounds:
Prairies and gardens and orchards,
Heathlands and plains and bosks.

3. Eu, las! cui Amors oblida,
   Que sui fors del dreih viatge,
   Agra de joi ma partida,
   Mas ira.m fai destorber;
   E no sai on me repona
   Pus mo joi me desazona;
   E no.m tenhatz per leuger
   S'eu dic alcu vilanatge.

I, alas! whom love forgets
Because I am off the straight path,
Would have of joy my part,
But grief disturbs me;
And I know not where to hide
When [grief] my joy destroys.
And do not consider me frivolous
If I say certain coarse things.

4. Una fausa deschauzida
   Traïritz de mal linhatge
   M'a traït et es traïda,
   E colh lo ram ab que.s fer;
   E can autre l'arazona,
   D'eus lo seu tort m'ochaizona;
   Et an ne mais li derrer
   Qu'eu, qui n'ai faih lonc badatge.

A false, rude
Traitress of bad lineage
Has betrayed me, and is herself betrayed,
And picks the branch with which she beats herself,
And when another speaks to her,
Of her own wrong she accuses him.
And from her the latecomers have more
Than I who have had a long wait.

5. Mout l'avia gen servida
   Tro ac vas mi cor volatge;
   E pus ilh no m'es cobida,
   Mout sui fols, si mais la ser.
   Servirs c'om no gazardona,
   Et esperansa bretona
   Fai de senhor escuder
   Per costum e per uzatge.

Much had I nobly served her
Until she had toward me a fickle heart;
And since she is not destined for me,
Much of a fool I am if I serve her more.
Service that one does not reward,
Like the Bretons' hope [for the return of King Arthur],
Makes a squire of a lord,
By custom and habit.

6. Pois tan es vas me falhida,
   Aisi lais so senhoratge,
   E no volh que.m si' aizida
   Ni ja mais parlar no.n quer.
   Mas pero qui m'en razona,
   La paraula m'en es bona,
   E m'en esjau volonter
   E.m n'alegre mo coratge.

Since she has so failed me,
I leave thus her domain
And do not want her to be near me,
Nor ever more do I seek to speak [to her].
But he who speaks to me of her,
His word is good to me,
And I enjoy it willingly,
And lighten with it my heart.

Example 35.

Bertran de Born (ca. 1140–1205),
Rassa, tant creis

Paris, B. N., f. frç. 22543 (Chansonnier d'Urfe), fol. 6d.

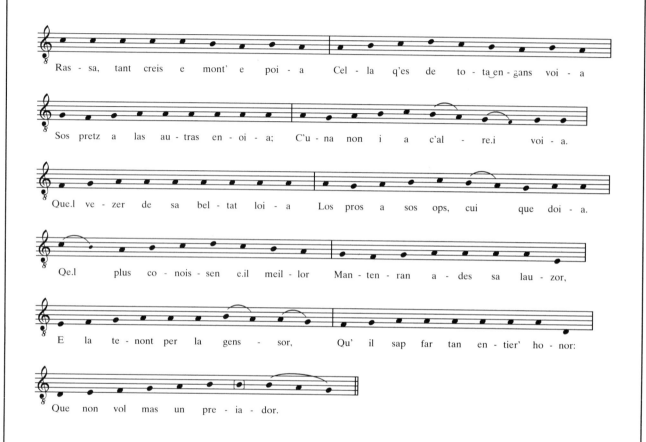

Ras - sa, tant creis e mont' e poi - a Cel - la q'es de to - ta en - gans voi - a

Sos pretz a las au - tras en - oi - a; C'u - na non i a c'al - re.i voi - a.

Que.l ve - zer de sa bel - tat loi - a Los pros a sos ops, cui que doi - a.

Qe.l plus co - nois - sen e.il meil - lor Man - ten - ran a - des sa lau - zor,

E la te - nont per la gens - sor, Qu' il sap far tan en - tier' ho - nor:

Que non vol mas un pre - ia - dor.

On the level of *amour courtoise*, Bertran is informing "Rassa" (the *senhal* or songname for his friend Count Geoffrey of Toulouse)—and whoever else is listening—that the unnamed lady prefers him, a minor noble, in spite of the attentions of much greater lords. These are identified in verse 2 by naming the territories they rule: Geoffrey of Brittany, Count Richard of Poitou, Raymond of Toulouse, and King Alfonso of Saragosa (Aragon). Bertran's poems generally operate on both an amorous and political level, and this becomes increasingly apparent as the poem progresses.

Example 35. Bertran de Born, *Rassa, tant creis*

The viscount in verse 5 is Aimer V of Limoges, who assisted in holding that city against the count, Richard. Maurin and Aigar are characters in a *chanson de geste*. The mariner in verse 6 may refer to Geoffrey, whose land of Brittany was renowned for its sailors, while the good warrior is Richard and the tourney goer the "young King" Henry, son of Henry II of England (and brother to Geoffrey and Richard—all relates to English-held lands in France). Golfier de Lastours is Bertran's nephew and a poet.

The five lines of the short sixth stanza should be sung to the last five phrases of music; the two-line envoy of stanza seven to the last two.

1. [Count] Rassa, so grows and rises and climbs
   She who is of all deceits void,
   [That] her prestige annoys the best,
   For not one has the power to harm her,
   Since the sight of her beauty binds
   The worthy to her cause, no matter who smarts.
   The most knowing and the best
   Maintain always her praise
   And consider her the most beautiful,
   Because she knows how to bestow such perfect honor,
   She does not want more than one suitor.

2. Rassa, als rics es orgoillosa,
   Et a gran sen a lei de tosa,
   Qui non vol Pietieus ni Tolosa
   Ni Bretaigna ni Serragosa.
   Anz es de pretz tant enveiosa
   Q'alz pros paubres es amorosa.
   Pois m'a pres per chastiador
   Prec la qu'il tengua car s'amor,
   Et am mais un pro vavassor
   Q'un comt' o duc galiador
   Que la tengues a desonor.

   Rassa, with the mighty she is proud,
   And she is very sensible in a young lady's way,
   Because she does not want Poitou or Toulouse
   Or Brittany or Saragossa.
   Rather, she is of merit so desirous
   That of the valiant poor she is amorous.
   Since she has taken me as her counselor,
   I pray to her that she may hold her love dear
   And love more a poor vavasor
   Than a count or treacherous duke,
   Because [then] I would hold her in dishonor.

3. Rassa, dompna q'es fresc'e fina,
   Coinda e gaia e mesquina,
   Pel saur ab color de robina,
   Blanca pel col cum flors d'espina,
   Coide mol ab dura tetina,
   E sembla conil de l'esquina,
   E a fina, fresca color,
   Ab bon pretz et ab gran lauzor,
   Leu podon triar l'i meillor
   Aquil qe.is fant conoissedor

   De mi, vas cal part q'ieu ador.

   Rassa, a lady I have who is fresh and fine,
   A pretty and gay young creature;
   [She has] blond hair with a sheen of ruby,
   White skin like the flower of hawthorne,
   Soft arms and firm breasts,
   And the supple back of a rabbit.
   By her fine fresh color,
   By her good fame and her praiseworthiness
   Easily they can discern her as the best
   Those who make themselves out to be
     knowledgeable
   About me [and about] where I direct my
     adoration.

Example 35. Bertran de Born, *Rassa, tant creis*

4. Rassa, rics hom que ren non dona,
   Ni acuoill ni met ni non sona,
   E qui senes tort ochaisona,

   E, qui merce.il qier, non perdona,
   M'enoia, e tota persona

   Qe servizi non guizerdona.
   E li ric home cassador
   M'enoiont, e.il buzatador,

   Gaban de volada d'austor;
   Ni ja mais d'armas ni d'amor
   Non parlaran mot entre lor.

Rassa, a man who gives nothing,
Does not invite or spend or celebrate,
And who, without [there being any] wrong,
   accuses,
And when asked for mercy, does not pardon,
[Such a man] annoys me, and [so does] any
   person
Who does not reward service.
And the mighty, hunters [all],
Annoy me, as do those who hunt with
   buzzards.
They boast of the flight of the hawk,
But never of weapons or love
Will they speak a word among themselves.

5. Rassa, aisso.us prec que vos plassa:
   Rics hom que de gerra no.is lassa,
   Ni no s'en laissa per menassa,
   Tro c'om se lais que mal no.il fassa,
   Val mais que ribieira ni cassa,
   Que bon pretz n'acuoill e n'amassa.
   Maurin e n'Agar, son seignor,
   Ten hom per bon envazidor.
   E.l vescoms defenda s'onor,
   E.l coms l'apelle per vigor,
   E veiam l'ades al pascor.

Rassa, this I beg, that it may please you:
A powerful man who does not tire of war
And does not shy from it for a menace
Until no one is left who could do him harm
Is worth more than river birds or prey,
Which brings and holds no great merit.
Maurin, with Aigar, his lord,
One considers a good invader.
May the viscount defend his honor,
May the count demand it of him by force,
And may we see him soon, at Easter!

6. Marinier, vos avetz honor,
   E nos avem camiat seignor
   Bon gerrier per torneiador.
   E prec a.n Golfier de la Tor
   Mos chantars no.il fassa paor.

Mariner, you have honor,
And we have changed a lord—
A good warrior—for a tourney goer.
And I beg of Golfier de Lastours
[That] my song may not give him a scare.

7. Papiol, mon chanter recor
   En la cort mon mal Belh Senhor.

Papiol, run through my song again
At the court of my naughty Fair Lord.

Example 36.
Arnaut Daniel (mid-twelfth century), *Lo ferm voler*

Milan, Bibl. Ambros., R71 sup., fol. 73.

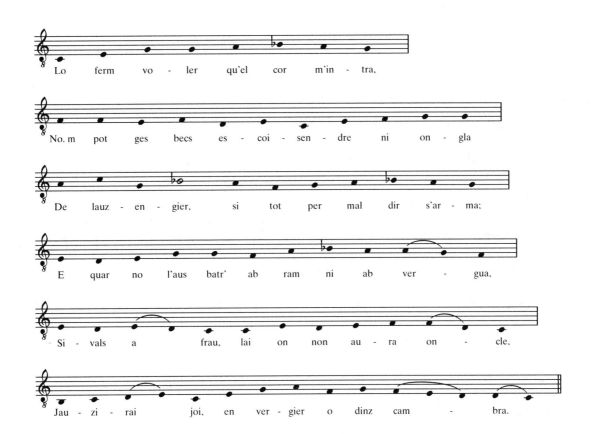

Lo ferm vo - ler qu'el cor m'in - tra,

No.m pot ges becs es - coi - sen - dre ni on - gla

De lauz - en - gier, si tot per mal dir s'ar - ma;

E quar no l'aus batr' ab ram ni ab ver - gua,

Si vals a frau, lai on non au - ra on - cle,

Jau - zi - rai joi, en ver - gier o dinz cam - bra.

Example 36. Arnaut Daniel, *Lo ferm voler*

1. The firm desire that into my heart enters,
   Cannot be torn from me by the beak or fingernail
   Of the slanderous gossiper, as such as he may arm himself to say evil;
   And since I dare not beat him with branch or rod,
   At least in secret, when I will have no [watchful] uncle,
   Will I rejoice in joy, in a garden or a chamber.

2. Quan mi soven de la cambra   When I recall the chamber
   On, al mieu dan, sai que nuils hom   Where, to my pain, I know no man
       non intra,   enters,—
   Ans mi son tug plus que fraire ni oncle, Rather, to me they are all more [hostile]
                                                  than brother or uncle—
   Non ai membre no.m fremisca, ni ongla,   I have no limb or fingernail which does
                                                  not tremble,
   Plus que non fai l'enfas denant la vergua; More so than does a child at the sight of
                                                  the rod;
   Tal pāor ai que.ill sia trop de m'arma. Such a fright I have that I am hers too
                                                  much with my soul.

3. Del cors li fos, non de l'arma!   In body would that I were hers, not in
                                                  soul,
   E cossentis m'a celat dinz sa cambra!   And would that she receive me secretly
                                                  in her chamber!
   Que plus me nafra.l cor que colps de   For it wounds my heart more than blows
       vergua,   of a rod
   Quar lo sieus sers, lai on ill es, non   That her servant, there where he is, does
       intra;   not enter;
   De lieis serai aisi com carns ez ongla, With her I shall be henceforth as flesh
                                                  and fingernail,
   E non creirai castic d'amie ni d'oncle. And I shall not believe the warning of
                                                  friend or uncle.

4. Anc la seror de mon oncle   Never the sister of my uncle
   Non amei tan ni plus, per aquest'arma!   Did I love so much or more, by this my
                                                  soul!
   Que tan vezis com es lo detz de l'ongla, For as close as is the finger to the nail,
   S'a lieis plagues, volgr'esser de sa   If it pleased her, would I like to be in
       cambra;   her chamber;
   De mi pot far l'amors qu'ins el cor   With me love, which enters my heart,
       m'intra   can have
   Mieils a son vol c'om fortz de frevol   Better its way than a strong man [can]
       vergua.   with a weak rod.

Example 36. Arnaut Daniel, *Lo ferm voler*

5. Pois floris la seca vergua,
   Ni d'En Adam foron nebot ni oncle,

   Tan fin'amors com cela qu'el cor
      m'intra
   Non cuig qu'anc fos en cors, ni eis
      en arma;
   On qu'ill estei, fors en plan o dinz
      cambra,
   Mos cors de lieis no.s part, tan com
      ten l'ongla.

6. C'aisi s'enpren e s'enongla

   Mos cors en lieis com l'escors'en
      la vergua;
   Qu'ill m'es de joi tors e palais e cambra,

   Ez am la mais no fas cozin ni oncle.

   Qu'en paradis n'aura doble joi m'arma,
   Si ja nuils hom per ben amar lai intra.

7. Arnautz tramer son chantar d'ongl'e
      d'oncle.
   Ab grat de lieis que de sa vergua l'arma,

   Son Dezirat, c'ab pretz en cambra intra.

Never since flowered the dry branch
And from Adam came forth nephew and
   uncle,
Such true love as that which enters my
   heart
Has been, I don't think, in body or even
   in soul;
Wherever she may be, out in the open or
   in her chamber,
My body from her does not depart by so
   much space as takes up a fingernail.

Holding on and clinging as with
   fingernails
To her, my body [is] like the bark on the
   branch;
For she is to me tower and palace and
   chamber of joy,
And I love her more than I do cousin or
   uncle.
In paradise will have double joy my soul,
If ever a man through good loving
   therein enters.

Arnaut transmits his song of fingernail
   and of uncle,
For the pleasure of her who arms him
   with her rod,
To his Desired Love, who with honor
   her chamber enters.

PART 6

Liber Sancti Jacobi

Example 37.
Master Walter of Castle Renard,
Regi perhennis (conductus)

Liber Sancti Jacobi, fol. 187

1. Re - gi per - hen - nis glo-ri - e sit can - ti cum
2. De - co - ra - vit Ys - pa - ni - am Ja - co - bus et

le - ti - ci - e.
Gal-li - ci - am;

Qui tri - um - phum vi-cto-ri - e
Il - lam - que gen-tem im-pi - am

Ja - co - bo de - dit ho - di - e.
Chri - ste fe - cit ec-cle - si - am.

1. To the King of eternal glory
   Be a song of gladness,
   Who did give a triumph of victory
   This day to James.

2. James adorned
   Spain and Galicia;
   And of that faithless people,
   O Christ, he made a church.

84

Example 38.

Master Goslen, Bishop of Soissons
(d. 1152), *Alleluia: Vocavit Jhesus Jacobum*

Liber Sancti Jacobi, fol. 119, 189'–190

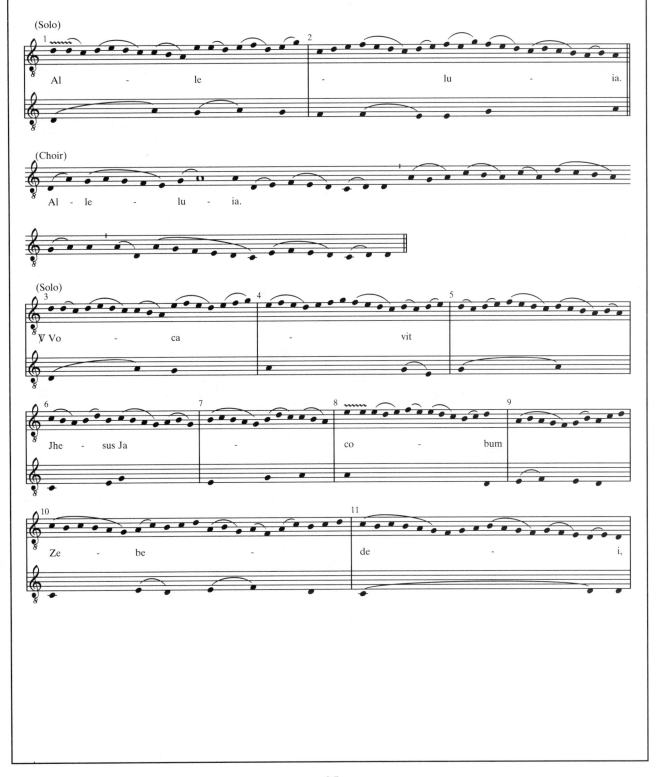

Example 38. Master Goslen, *Alleluia: Vocavit Jhesus Jacobum*

Alleluia.
  Jesus called James, son of Zebedee, and John his brother:
  And gave them the name Boanerges, which means Sons of Thunder.
Alleluia.

PART 7

Parisian Sacred Music

Example 39.

Alleluia: Adorabo ad templum
(organum duplum)
Comparative versions:

A. Version in Wolfenbüttel, Herzog August-Bibliothek, Helm. 677 (W_1), fol. 30

B. Version in Florence, Bib. Laurenziana, Pluteus 29.1 (*F*), fol. 107–8

C. Version in Wolfenbüttel, Herzog August-Bibliothek, Helm. 1206 (W_2), fol. 70′–71

D. Substitute clausulae from *F*

Rhythmically free *organum purum* sections are notated in nonrhythmic black noteheads; lines above individual notes (𝅝) are an editorial suggestion of a possible lengthening of the note according to the rules of consonance. Copula and discant sections are given in rhythmic notation, but with bar lines still used to indicate phrase length. Plicas are shown by small notes in *organum purum* and by a diagonal line through the stem in copula and discant. Ligatures are shown by square brackets (⌐—¬), and currentes (▰◆) by a slur (⌒).

Motet texts that were subsequently added to some of the discant sections, converting them into motets, are given in small print for reference purposes. Notational variants in the motet versions are shown through the use of small notes.

The original plainchant is given above as Anthology Example 5.

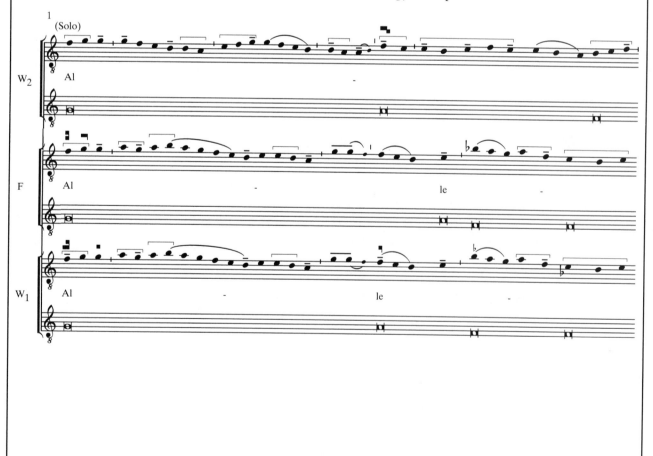

Example 39. *Alleluia: Adorabo ad templum*

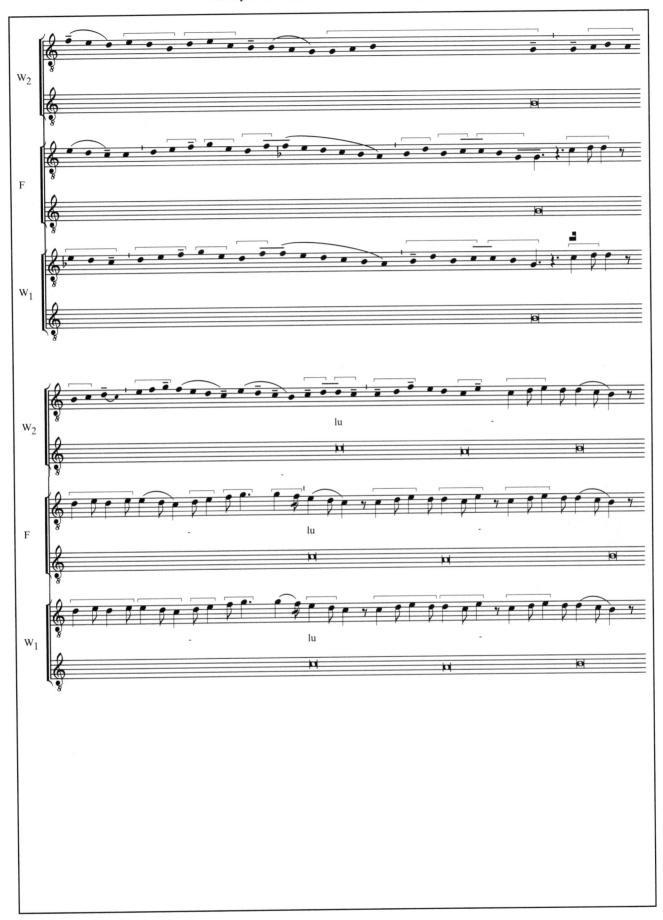

89

Example 39. Alleluia: Adorabo ad templum

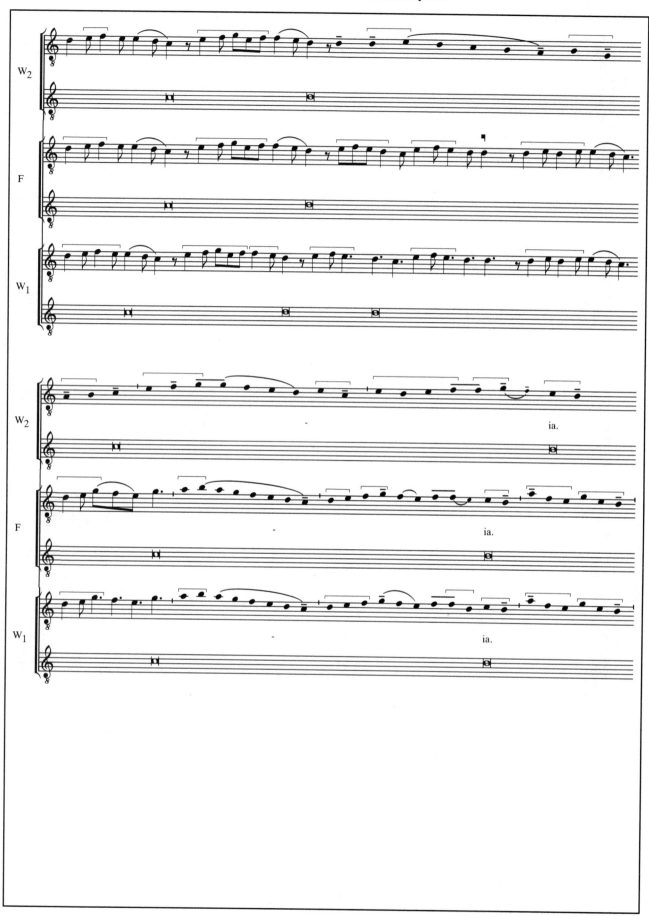

Example 39. *Alleluia: Adorabo ad templum*

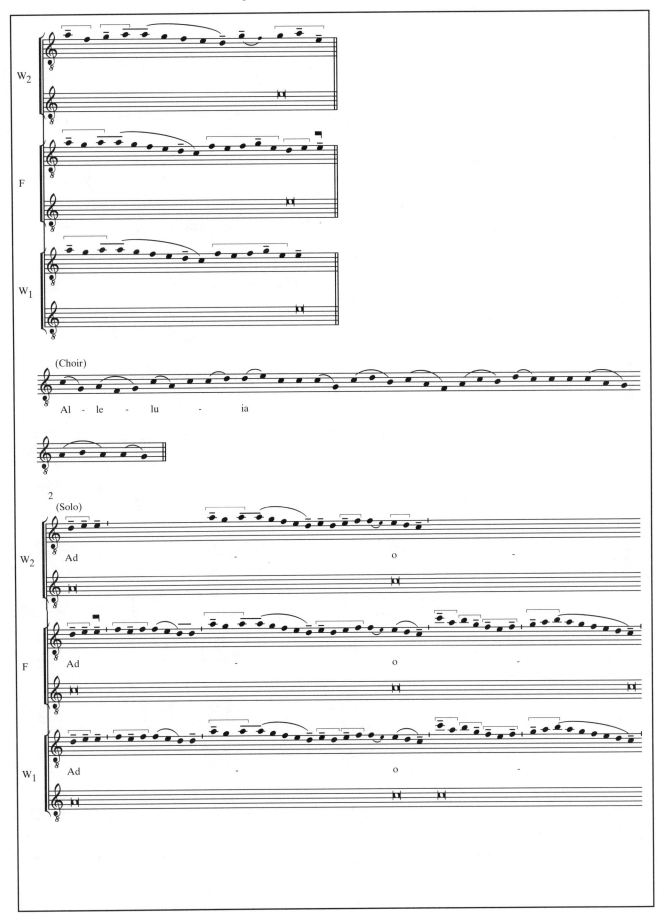

Example 39. *Alleluia: Adorabo ad templum*

Substitute clausula

From F, fol. 181

92

Example 39. *Alleluia: Adorabo ad templum*

Example 39. *Alleluia: Adorabo ad templum*

94

Example 39. *Alleluia: Adorabo ad templum*

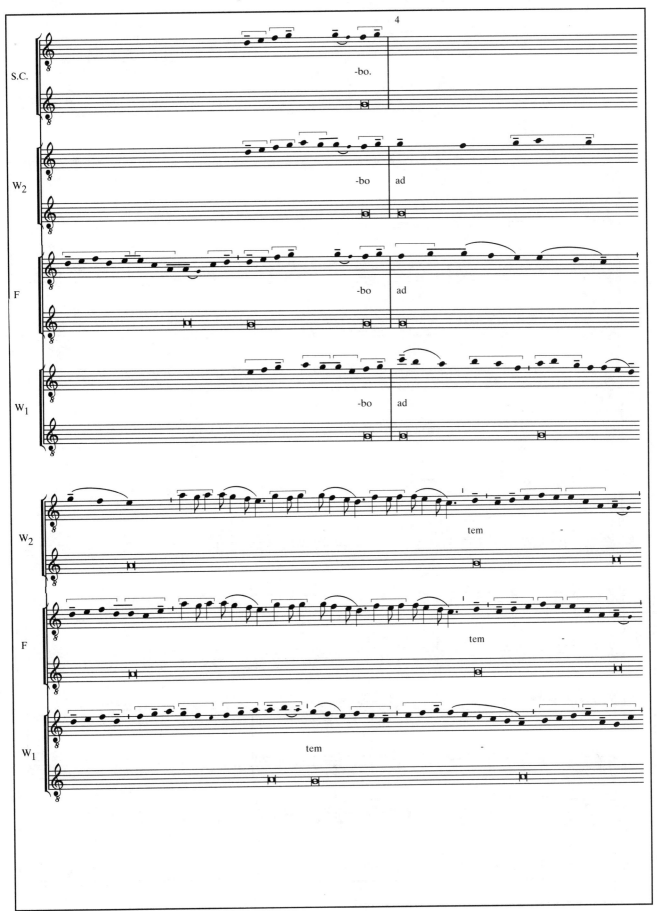

95

Example 39. *Alleluia: Adorabo ad templum*

96

Example 39. *Alleluia: Adorabo ad templum*

97

Example 39. *Alleluia: Adorabo ad templum*

* Substitute two-voice clausula, *F*, fol. 154'   Motetus text from *W₂*, fol. 157   Added triplum, *Hu*, fol. 114

Example 39. Alleluia: Adorabo ad templum

an - ge - lo - rum, Sub - le - va - trix cor - di - um, Fir - ma spes

i - ni - ti - o, Ir - ri - gu - a ro - ris au - xi - li - o

*[Tra-vail-le du mau d'a-mer En-pen - sant Che-vau - chai en un des -

fi te - [Lo-cus hic ter - ri - bi - lis, Sa-cra - tus, Mun-dus ve - ne - ra - bi -

* Latin motet text, troping the tenor, *F*, fol. 406'–407
Later French secular text, *Mo*, fol. 248–248'

Example 39. *Alleluia: Adorabo ad templum*

Example 39. Alleluia: Adorabo ad templum

101

Example 39. Alleluia: Adorabo ad templum

102

Example 39. *Alleluia: Adorabo ad templum*

103

Example 39. *Alleluia: Adorabo ad templum*

Example 39. *Alleluia: Adorabo ad templum*

S.C. Re - mo-vens ex - si - li - um, In na - ti tu - i iu - di - ci - um.

nos so - la per fi - li - um, Spes fi - de - li um.]

Example 39. *Alleluia: Adorabo ad templum*

Version W₁ and W₂ repeat the initial *Alleluia*.
Version F has a new, shorter organal setting in place of a da capo.

Example 39. *Alleluia: Adorabo ad templum*

al - le - lu - ia

(Choir)

Tenor text

Alleluia:
I will worship toward thy holy temple:
And I will confess thy name.
Alleluia.

Section 6: Motetus text later added to W₂ discant clausula section

(*F Motet 2,24, fol. 406'–407*)

Locus hic terribilis,	How dreaful is this place,
Sacratus,	Consecrated
Mundus venerabilis,	Pure, venerable,
Ornatus,	Adorned,
Iubilis,	Joyful,
Fundo petre stabilis,	Stable, founded on a rock,
Firmatus	Extended
Per longitudinem	By the longitude
Tenditur fidei,	Of faith,
Per altitudinem	Elevated
Erigitur	By the altitude
Spei	Of hope,
Habens latitudinem,	Having a latitude,
Qua diffunditur	By which it is spread out
A mare proximi	From the bordering sea;
Et Dei	And, therefore,
Igitur	Of God;
Ut in hac ecclesia	So that in this church
Bene placeam	I might be well pleasing
Ei,	To him,
Deleam	I will forsake
Vitia	Sins,
Et confitebor.	*And I will confess.*

Example 39. *Alleluia: Adorabo ad templum*

Section 6: Later French secular text added to the same clausula

(Mo motet 6,211, fol. 248–248')

Traveillié du mau d'amer	Tortured by the pain of loving,
Enpensant	Thinking,
Chevauchai en un destour,	I was riding in a secluded place,
Ma dolour	Alleviating my sorrow.
Alejant	Such weather
Tel tens fist com en pascor;	It was as at Easter;
Sanz pastor	Without a shepherd,
Truis pastore avenant,	I found a shepherdess
Seant lés un aubour;	Sitting next to a tree;
Mès mount ot povre atour.	Wearing simple clothing.
Vers li m'ator:	Toward her I turned:
Peour ot;	She was afraid;
Si quelli son atour;	She gathered up her clothing
Si s'en ala atant.	And went away quickly.
Je sui tout errant;	Everywhere I followed her:
Maintenant	Now
En terour	Into terror
La mis et en freour;	I put her and into fright,
Si mua coulour:	So her color changed:
Talent	The desire
D'estreindre m'ardour	To put out my ardour
Oi plus que devant.	Was stronger than before.

Section 6: Motetus text added to the two-voice substitute clausula of F

(W₂, Motet 2,24, fol. 157)

De virgula, veris initio,	From a little stem, at the beginning of spring,
Irrigua roris auxilio,	Watered by the aid of the dew,
Flos oritur in hoc exsilio.	A flower grew in this place of exile.
Angelico nuntio,	By the salutation
Salutatorio,	Of the angelic messenger,
Fructificat mater in filio	The mother bore fruit in the Son
Virginei pudoris nulla fit lesio.	With no ruin of her virgin chastity.
Deluditur visus et ratio,	Sight and reason are deluded
Dum nascitur rosa de lilio	When the rose is born from the lily
O floridum celi rosarium!	O florid rose garden of heaven!
O lilium!	O lily!
O vite balsamum!	O balsam of life!
Adiuva nos sola per filium,	Thou alone help us by thy Son,
Spes fidelium.	Hope of the faithful.

Example 39. *Alleluia: Adorabo ad templum*

Section 6: *Triplum text and voice added to the foregoing two-voice motet*

(*Hu, motet no. 25, fol. 114*)

O Maria, decus angelorum,	O Mary, glory of the angels,
Sublevatrix cordium,	Uplifter of hearts,
Firma spes fidelium,	Firm hope of the faithful,
Mater es humilium	Thou art mother of the humble,
Ad te supplicantium,	Suppliant to thee.
Consolatrix gentium,	Consoler of the nations,
Nobis da solacium.	Grant us comfort.
Dele nostrum vitium,	Remove our sin,
Dele luctus omnium,	Remove the grief of all,
Nobis ad remedium	[Grant] us a remedy
Exorando filium.	By interceding with the Son.
In beate gremium	Gather us in thy blessed embrace,
Nos colloces, sordium	Remove the exile
Removens exsilium,	Of the outcasts,
In nati tui iudicium.	At the judgment seat of thy Son.

Example 40.

Perotin, *Alleluia: Posui adiutorium*
(organum triplum)

Florence, Bib. Laurenziana, Pluteus 29.1 (F), fols. 36–37′.

110

Example 40. Perotin, *Alleluia: Posui adiutorium*

Example 40. Perotin, *Alleluia: Posui adiutorium*

112

Example 40. Perotin, *Alleluia: Posui adiutorium*

Example 40. Perotin, *Alleluia: Posui adiutorium*

114

Example 40. Perotin, *Alleluia: Posui adiutorium*

de ple - be me - a.

Alleluia:
   I have laid help upon a mighty one:
   And exalted one chosen from my people.
Alleluia.

Example 41.

Veste nuptiali (monophonic conductus simplex)

Florence, Bibl. Laur., Pluteus 29.1 (F), fol. 450'.

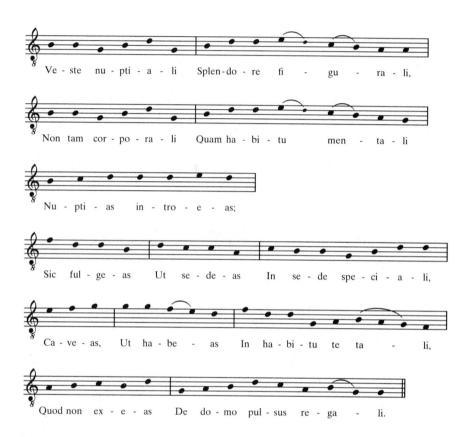

Ve - ste nu - pti - a - li Splen-do - re fi - gu - ra - li,

Non tam cor - po - ra - li Quam ha - bi - tu men - ta - li

Nu - pti - as in - tro - e - as;

Sic ful - ge - as Ut se - de - as In se - de spe - ci - a - li,

Ca - ve - as, Ut ha - be - as In ha - bi - tu te ta - li,

Quod non ex - e - as De do - mo pul - sus re - ga - li.

Example 41. *Veste nuptiali*

The text, by Philip the Chancellor, concerns the parable of the wise and foolish virgins.

1. In a wedding garment
   Of symbolic splendor,
   Not so much of bodily
   As of mental raiment,
   Go in unto the wedding feast.
   Thus let you sit
   In a special seat.
   Beware
   That you wear
   Such a garment;
   That you do not depart,
   Expelled from the royal house.

2. Virgo clamat foris
   In tenebris meroris;
   Vana vox clamoris
   Non est mentis sed oris;
   Ei clausa ianua,
   Nam fatua
   Cum vacua
   Stat lampade splendoris;
   Non, sua,
   Sat mutua,
   Prudens plena timoris,
   Ne residua
   Non sufficiens liquoris.

   A virgin cries outside
   In the darkness of sorrow.
   The vain voice of crying
   Is not of the mind, but of the mouth.
   To her, the door is closed;
   For, foolish,
   With a lamp
   Empty of light, she stands
   With not enough
   For both,
   The wise one is full of fear
   That what remains of the oil
   Is not enough.

3. Germen sine flore,
   Framis sine dulcore,
   Vas sine liquore,
   Vox est sine stentore;
   Sed que cum lampadibus
   Ardentibus
   In manibus
   In operum candore,
   Floribus
   Patentibus
   Intrant absque clamore,
   Cibus talibus
   Refici mente non ore.

   A stem without a flower,
   Hunger without sweetness,
   A vessel without fluid,
   Is a voice without sound.
   But they who with lamps
   Burning
   In their hands,
   In the radiance of their deeds,
   With flowers,
   Unhindered
   Enter without crying;
   And the food for such
   Is refreshment for the mind, not the mouth.

Example 42.
O *curas hominum* (monophonic conductus cum cauda)

Florence, Bib. Laur., Pluteus 29.1 (*F*), fol. 424′.

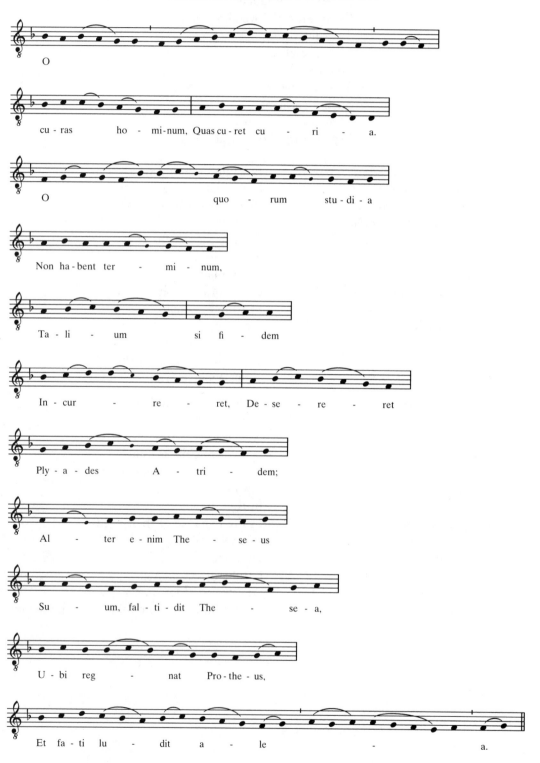

O

cu - ras   ho - mi - num, Quas cu - ret cu - ri - a.

O   quo - rum   stu - di - a

Non ha - bent ter - mi - num,

Ta - li - um   si fi - dem

In - cur - re - ret, De - se - re - ret

Ply - a - des   A - tri - dem;

Al - ter e - nim The - se - us

Su - um, fal - ti - dit The - se - a,

U - bi reg - nat Pro - the - us,

Et fa - ti lu - dit a - le - a.

Example 42. *O curas hominum*

An *admonitio* criticizing the greed of the papal court, where high position and forgiveness of sin can be bought and he who has no money has no chance of advancement.

1. O the cares of men
   Which the curia deals with!
   O their labors
   Without end!
   If the trustworthiness
   Of such as they
   He should encounter,
   Plyades would forsake
   Atrides;
   Theseus and Thesea
   Would tire
   Of one another,
   Where Proteus reigns
   And gambles with fate.

2. Ab aula principis,   From the court of the prince,
   Si nihil habeas,   If you have nothing,
   Oportet abeas;   You must depart.
   Spem vanam concipis,   You imagine a vain hope,
   Tenuis   O slender
   Fortuna.   Fortune!
   Omnimoda   Always
   Ad commoda   On gains
   Hominum mens una;   The minds of men are set.
   A quo nil umungitur,   He who does not cheat
   Opus perdit et operam;   Wastes his work and trouble.
   Quod habenti dabitur,   "To him that hath, it shall be given"
   Tenent omnes ad literam.   All hold quite literally.

3. In lucrum vertitur   The lightness of censure
   Censurae levitas;   Is turned into profit;
   Fracta securitas   Broken security
   Danti remittitur,   Is forgiven the giver.
   Explicas   You may expound
   Decreta   The laws
   Ad libitum,   As you like,
   Si sonitum   If money
   Dederit moneta.   Has spoken.
   Plenis aere sacculis   By purses full of coin
   Rei poena minuitur,   The punishment of the guilty is diminished.
   Locum dic a loculis   *Place* comes from *pockets*,
   Unde locus si quaeritur.   If one wants to know what *position* means.

Example 43.

Omnes gentes (monophonic rondellus)

Florence, Bib. Laur., Pluteus 29.1 (F), fol. 465.

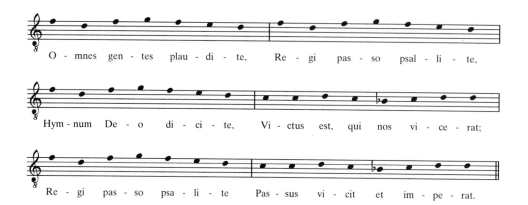

O - mnes gen - tes plau - di - te, Re - gi pas - so psal - li - te,

Hym - num De - o di - ci - te, Vi - ctus est, qui nos vi - ce - rat;

Re - gi pas - so psa - li - te Pas - sus vi - cit et im - pe - rat.

1. O clap your hands, all ye people,
   Sing songs to the crucified king,
   Chant a hymn to God,
   For he was conquered, who had conquered us;
   Sing songs to the crucified king,
   For, crucified, he conquers and reigns.

2. Suspensus in stipite,   Hung from the tree,
   Regi passo psallite,   *Sing songs to the crucified king,*
   Occisus immerite   And, unjustly killed,
   Restaurat, quod perierat;   He restores what had been lost;
   Regi passo psallite,   *Sing songs to the crucified king,*
   Passus vicit et imperat.   *For, crucified, he conquers and reigns.*

3. Laudem Deo canite,   Sing praises to God,
   Regi passo psallite,   *Sing songs to the crucified king,*
   Libertatis perdite   Who reopens for his people
   Qui viam suis reserat;   The way of lost liberty;
   Regi passo psallite,   *Sing songs to the crucified king,*
   Passus vicit et imperat.   *For, crucified, he conquers and reigns.*

Example 44.

Ver pacis asperit (two-voice conductus simplex)

Florence, Bibl. Laur., Pluteus 29.1 (*F*), fol. 355.

The earliest datable polyphonic conductus. The text was written by Walter of Chatillon for the coronation of King Philip Augustus at Reims in 1179.

121

Example 44. *Ver pacis asperit*

1. The springtime of peace opens
   The womb of the earth,
   It has discovered an oarsman
   Of safety for Rheims.
   Now Peter has drawn
   Both swords
   By which will be driven off
   The invasion of her enemies.

2. Cui plus contulerit
   Natura sapere,
   Quam plus exulerit
   Honoris onere,
   Qui magis noverit
   Sibi disponere.
   Que vox, que poterit
   Lingua vetexere?

   Him on whom Nature
   Has conferred more wisdom
   She burdens yet more
   With the weight of honor.
   One who knows better
   Has to dispose matters for his people,
   What voice, what tongue
   Can disclose?

3. In unum confluit
   Totus fons gratie,
   Cuius ros imbuit
   Rus conscientie,
   Rivum, quem genuit
   Rigor justitie,
   Flumen preterfluit
   Misericordie.

   In one man flows together
   The whole spring of grace,
   Whose dew moistens
   The soil of conscience;
   The stream which the rigor
   Of justice has begotten
   Is accompanied
   By the river of mercy.

4. Patet ad oculum
   Facta translatio,
   Ut per avunculum
   Sororis filio,
   Gratie cumulum
   Propinet unctio,
   Que per miraculum
   Datur Remigio.

   It is clear to the eye,
   The transfer is done,
   So that by the uncle,
   Upon the sister's son,
   The anointing bestows
   The total sum of graces,
   Which by a miracle
   Was granted to Remigius.

5. Flens in miseriis
   Urbs Senonensium
   Patebit impiis
   Per hoc divortium
   Patres cum filiis,
   Genus egregium
   Ceduntur gladiis
   More bidentium.

   Weeping in miseries,
   The city of Sens
   Will be open to the impious
   Through this separation;
   Fathers with their sons,
   A noble race,
   Are slain by swords,
   Like sacrificial sheep.

Example 45.

Quod promisit ab eterno (two-voice conductus cum cauda)

Wolfenbüttel, Herzog August-Bibl., Helm. 677 (W₁), fol. 139′.

Example 45. *Quod promisit ab eterno*

Example 45. *Quod promisit ab eterno*

125

Example 45. *Quod promisit ab eterno*

126

Example 45. *Quod promisit ab eterno*

1. What he promised from eternity
    The Father in a day fulfills today,
    Sending from on high his Word
    Into Edom.

2. A cloud, light and living,
    The pure, virginal flesh
    Rains down upon us
    A plenitude of spiritual dew.

3. Once there was a sign
    Signifying the clothing of the Word:
    A cloud, bringing the aid
    Of light and of shade.

Example 46.

A solis ortus cardine (three-voice conductus cum cauda)

Florence, Bibl. Laur., Pluteus 29.1 (*F*), fols. 242′–43′.

Example 46. A solis ortus cardine

129

Example 46. A *solis ortus cardine*

Example 46. A solis ortus cardine

From the sun's rising
Proceeded the sun's ray,
When appearing in man,
The Son, sent from the Father,
Chose, without seed,
To be born, a virgin from a virgin,
And, standing in our midst,
Although he knew not eclipse,
Those enveloped in darkness,
He looked upon with new light;
Death, which the messenger of death
Had established for sin,
He condemned by his own blood,
And returned to the better
Whatever was worse.

PART 8

The Early Motet

Example 47.

Virgo plena gratie — Go

A. Source clausula

Wolfenbüttel, Herzog August-Bibl., Helm 677 (W₁), fol. 54.

B. Single-texted three-voice motet

Wolfenbüttel, Herzog August-Bibl., Helm. 1206 (W₂), fol. 129′–130, with reference to W₂, fol. 154′–55, and Florence, Bib. Laur., Pluteus 29.1 (F), fols. 393–93′.

The tenor is taken from the second syllable of *virgo* (Virgin) from the Gradual for the Feast of the Assumption of the Blessed Virgin Mary, August 15. The motet text tropes this in subject matter and in quotation at beginning and end.

Example 47. *Virgo plena gratie*—Go

Example 47. *Virgo plena gratie — Go*

Example 47. *Virgo plena gratie—Go*

Example 47. *Virgo plena gratie—Go*

Virgin full of grace,
Treasury of bounty,
Eye of clemency,
Pupil of affection,
Open door of mercy,
Ladder of charity,
Oil of gladness,
Name of sweetness;
Thou the familiar song
Guiding the sailor;
All things cry,
"Come to aid, O Mary!"
The times press on,
The last hour
Weighs upon us.
Shorten
These toilsome Egyptian days,
For the sake of thy sons,
O kind Virgin Mother.

Example 48.

A. *O Maria, maris stella—Veritatem* (single-texted three-voice motet)

Wolfenbüttel, Herzog August-Bibl., Helm. 1206 (W₂), fols. 125–25′.

B. *O Maria virgo—O Maria, maris stella—Veritatem* (double motet)

Montpellier, Fac. de med., H 196 (Mo), fols. 88′–90.

The irregular notation at the end of this version is a scribal indication of a ritard, discussed by theorists, but only occasionally shown in notation. Other instances are Examples 51 and 52.

Example 48. *O Maria, maris stella—Veritatem; O Maria virgo—O Maria, maris stella—Veritatem*

Example 48. O Maria, maris stella—Veritatem; O Maria virgo—O Maria, maris stella—Veritatem

O Maria virgo

O Mary, Davidic maiden,
Flower of virgins, only hope,
Way of compassion,
Light of grace,
Mother of mercy;
Thou alone ruleth in the heavenly arc;
The militia obey thee.
Thou alone sittest upon the throne of glory,
Illustrious, full of divine grace.
The stars are astonished by thy face,
The sun, the moon, by thy power,
All of which lamps,
At noonday,
Thou, by thy face,
Surpassest.
Pray mollify thy Son,
Whose daughter, in a wondrous way, thou art;
Lest we be judged adversely.
But grant the reward of eternal life.

O Maria, maris stella

O Mary, star of the sea,
Full of grace,
Mother and maiden,
Vessel of purity,
Temple of our Redeemer,
Sun of righteousness,
Gate of heaven, hope of the guilty,
Throne of glory,
Bather of the suffering,
Stream of compassion;
Hear thy servants pleading,
O Mother of grace,
That their sins may be washed away
Through thee today,
Who praise thee with a pure heart
In truth.

Example 49.
Quant je parti—Tuo (two-voice motet)

Montpellier, Fac. de med., H 196 (Mo), fols. 242'–43.

Mo: Quant je par - ti de m'a mi - e, Si li dis, qu'en des - con - fort

T: Tuo

Se - roi - e tou - te ma vie. Mes li a - mo - ros re - cort

Du sou - las et du de - port Et de sa grant cor - toi - si - e

En tout les maus, que je port. Mais ce me gre - va trop fort.

Quant vint a la de - par - ti - e, Et je dis: "A Diu, a - mi - e!"

Plou - rer la vi: Si m'a mort.

Example 49. *Quant je parti—Tuo*

When I departed from my friend,
I told her that in discomfort
I would be all my life.
But the lover derives comfort
From the pleasure and joy
And her great courtesy
In all the sufferings I bear.
But it grieved me much.
When came [the time of] separation,
And I said: "Adieu, my love."
I saw her cry: thus, she killed me.

Example 50.

Veni, virgo—Veni, sancte—Neuma
(double motet)

Montpellier, Fac. de med., H 196 (Mo), fols. 92′–93.

Tr: Ve - ni, vir - go be - a - tis - si - ma, Ve - ni, ma - ter

Mo: Ve - ni, san - cte spi - ri - tus, Ve - ni, lux gra - ti - e,

T: Neuma

ho - ne - stis - si - ma, E - sto no - bis sem - per pro - xi -

Ve - ni, re - ple ce - li - tus Tu - e fa - mi - li - e

ma, De - i ge - ni - trix pi - a, O Ma - ri -

Pe - cto - ra ra - di - ci - tus, Pa - ter po - ten - ci - e,

a! Nos cla - ri - fi - ca, Nos pu - ri - fi -

Et ex - tir - pa pe - ni - tus La - bem ne - qui - ci - e.

146

Example 50. *Veni, virgo—Veni, sancte—Neuma*

ca;   O - ra fi - li - um tu - um Pro no - bis, do - mi -

Da no - bis di - vi - ni - tus, pa - ter, sic vi - ve - re,

na,   Ut cun - cta fi - de - li - um Te - rat pec - ca - mi -

Ut te De - um co - le - re Et te pa - trem di - li - ge - re Pos -

na,   Con - fe - rens su - per - na gau - di - a

si - mus sem - per sin - ce - re   Et su - per - na

Per te, ce - li re - gi - na.

gau - di - a pos - si - de - re.

Example 50. *Veni, virgo—Veni, sancte—Neuma*

Triplum

Come, Virgin most blessed,
Come, mother most noble,
Be always near to us,
O kind mother of God,
O Mary!
Clarify us;
Purify us;
Pray thy Son
For us, o lady,
That He would cleanse
All the faults of the faithful,
Bestowing heavenly joys
Through you, queen of heaven.

Motetus

Come, Holy Spirit,
Come, Light of Grace,
Come, fill from heaven
Thy family's
Bosom utterly,
Father of might,
And totally eradicate
The stain of wickedness.
Grant us, O Father, divinely so to live,
That we may be always able with sincerity
To worship thee as God,
And love thee as Father,
And possess supernal joys.

Example 51.

En non Diu—Quant voi—Eius in oriente
(double motet)

Montpellier, Fac. de med., H 196 (Mo), fols. 145'–46.

Example 51. *En non Diu—Quant voi—Eius in oriente*

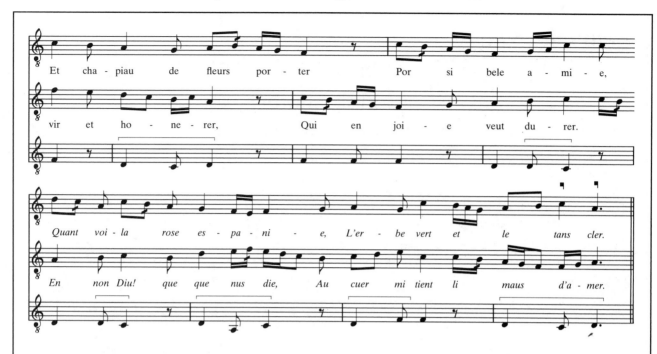

Triplum

In the name of God, whatever anyone may say,
When I see the green grass and the clear weather
And the nightingale singing,
Then sweet love asks me
Softly to sing about love's pleasure:
"Marion, let Robin love me!"
Well must I now exert myself
And wear a hat of flowers
For such a beautiful friend,
When I see the rose opening,
The green grass and the clear weather.

Motetus

When I see the rose opening,
The green grass and the clear weather
And the nightingale singing,
Then sweet love urges me
To make joy and rejoice,
For he who does not love, does not live.
Therefore one must exert oneself
To have love for a friend
And serve and honor [her]
Who wants to remain in joy.
In the name of God, whatever anyone may say,
In my heart I hold the pain of loving.

Example 52.

Trop sovent—Brunete—In seculum
(double motet)

Montpellier, Fac. de med., H 196 (*Mo*), fols. 124′–25.

Tr: Trop so - vent me dueil Et sui en gri - e - té, Et tou por ce -

Mo: Bru - nete, a qui j'ai mon cuer do - né. Por viz ai maint greif mal

T: In seculum

li Qui j'ai tant a - mé, Par son grant or - gueil Et par

en - du - ré. Por Deu! pre - gne vos de moi pi - té, Fins cuers

sa fier - té. *A ma dame ai mis mon cuer et mon pen - sé.*

a - mo - rous. *De de - bo - nai - re - té Vient a - mors.*

151

Example 52. *Trop sovent—Brunete—In seculum*

Triplum

Too often I lament
And am in grief—
And all for her
Whom I loved so much—
Because of her great pride
And her haughtiness.
To my lady I have given
My heart and my thinking.

Motetus

Brunete, to whom I have given my heart,
For you I have badly endured many a grief.
For God's sake, may you take pity on me,
Noble loving heart,
From kindliness
Comes love.

PART 9

The Continental Motet in the Late Thirteenth Century

Example 53.

Tout solas—Bone amour—Ne me blasmes mie
(conservative motet on a French tenor)

Montpellier, Fac. de med., H 196 (Mo), fols. 367'–68'.

Tr: Tout so - las et tou - te joi - e Vient de par a - mours a - mer: Ri - ce - ment son tans em - ploi - e Et bien doit chan - ter, Li de - duire et de - por - ter, Qui sans fau - ser sert a - mour, Et en ser - vant tant de - sert Par bien ou - vrer Que sa

Mo: Bone a - mour, qui les siens doc - trine et a - prent Et fait vivre en joie et en jou - vent, M'a don - né ta - lent A ces - te foys de chan - ter li - e - ment; Et je qui tous jours o - be - ir Veul a son com - man - de - ment, Chan - te - rai ren - voi -

T: NE ME BLASMES MIE

154

Example 53. *Tout solas—Bone amour—Ne me blasmes mie*

155

Example 53. *Tout solas — Bone amour — Ne me blasmes mie*

Triplum

All pleasure and all joy
Comes from loving a lover:
Richly employs his time
And must sing well,
Please and entertain her,
He who without falseness serves love,
And by serving he deserves,
As well as by working well,
That his lady deigns to call him her friend.
This is very much a sweet and gracious name
To call
And very sweet to hear.
By God! Will I ever see the day
When my lady deigns to call me that?

Motetus

Good love, which instructs and teaches its followers
And [lets them] live in joy and rejoicing,
Has given me the desire
At this time to sing happily;
And I, who always wish
To obey its command,
Will sing gaily
For the beautiful [lady] with the nice body
Whom I love so loyally
That my noble heart has no other intention
But to think about how
I can serve her
And love [her] always so fully
That sometimes she will look at me sweetly.

Example 54.

J'ai mis—Je n'en puis—Puerorum
(Franconian motet)

Montpellier, Fac. de med., H 196 (Mo), fols. 275′–77′.

Tr: J'ai mis tou-te ma pen-se-e lonc tans En a-mour loi-au-ment ser-vir, En-co-re veul je bien o-be-ïr A son com-mant, Ne pour quant Je n'en puis jo-ïr. Tant ne fait de mal sou-frir Ce-le que j'aim, que je ne sai Qui puis es de-ve-

Mo: Je n'en puis mais se je ne chant sou-vent, Car en mon cuer n'a se tris-tre-ce non. A-mours m'a-saut nuit

T: Puerorum

157

Example 54. *J'ai mis—Je n'en puis—Puerorum*

158

Example 54. *J'ai mis — Je n'en puis — Puerorum*

Example 54. *J'ai mis—Je n'en puis—Puerorum*

Example 54. *J'ai mis—Je n'en puis—Puerorum*

Triplum

I have put all my thought[s] for a long time
Into serving love loyally,
And I still wish to obey
Its command.
However, I cannot enjoy it,
So much makes me suffer with pain
She whom I love, so that I don't know
What is to become of me:
She causes trembling and shaking
In me and changes of color.
Often I cry and sigh,
And I cannot fault myself for loving her.
Alas! so much I desire her
That I know full well
That in the end for her love I will have to die
If no comfort I receive
From her, for too cruelly
Has she for a long time made me languish.
Hey! lady with the fair face,
Help me, your loyal friend,
If that is your pleasure,
For of the pain I feel
And have felt,
Nobody but you can cure me.
I beg you: [have] mercy,
For a single kind glance,
If I saw it coming from you,
Would comfort me
And give me hope
Of recovering joy,
Otherwise I fear I'll die,
For if pity
Or love will not work for me,
I cannot attain [that hope].

Example 54. *J'ai mis—Je n'en puis—Puerorum*

Motetus

I can stand it no longer if
I do not sing often,
For in my heart there is
But sadness.
Love assails me
Night and day so fiercely
That I have no hope,
Comfort or remedy.
In her prison
Has held me for a long time
She whom I love,
And she minds not at all
To grieve me
Continuously without reason.
God! she can find no other wrong
Than the fact that I love her too much:
Bad is the recompense
She gives me:
Now I know for sure
That I will never receive,
Since I love loyally,
The gift of her love.

Example 55.

Amours qui—Solem justicie—Solem
(Petronian motet)

Montpellier, Fac. de med., H 196 (Mo), fols. 328–29′ with variants from fols. 390–91′.

The main version given is that of Mo 7, 289, with significant variants from Mo 8, 338 shown on an added staff. Of particular interest are the seemingly anomalous measures 40 and 48 of Mo 7 where, during rapid declamation, four or five breves are notated instead of the usual three per *perfection* or measure. Although a possible scribal error, it may also be a suggestion of performance nuance: the addition of one or two extra breves is the only means available to the thirteenth-century scribe to indicate a broadening or ritard (see the final cadences of Examples 49b, 51, and 52). There is nothing in the lower voices here to prevent such a possibility.

Example 55. *Amours qui—Solem justicie—Solem*

Example 55. *Amours qui—Solem justicie—Solem*

165

Example 55. *Amours qui—Solem justicie—Solem*

166

Example 55. *Amours qui—Solem justicie—Solem*

Triplum

Love, which is my master, makes me sing:
So I shall sing and rejoice
About the love [I feel] for the simple silent one
Whom I dare not name
Because of the evil gossipers
(Whom may God send grief!).
But in my song,
Since I do not dare go to her,
I beg her to deign call me friend:
Then I will be able to double my joy
And rejoice mightily.

And if she does not do it, I will have to
Cry all my life,
Without any help
And without any deliverance
That one may find within a hundred years.
Hey! my good love, by your frankness
Into which I have put my desire,
I beg you to hurry
And put a spark
Of your fire under your breast
To light the fire;
For I do not know a better
Pleader to find in this cause,
Nor [anyone] who would know so perfectly how to proceed;
And, if he so pleases, such a reward
As he seems fit to attribute at his discretion,
I am and will be, without a thought of error.

Motetus

O Virgin, pure before and after,
Who wilt bear
The sun of righteousness,
The gate of gladness,
The King,
The inner source of purity;
O innocent cell,
Brightness of the sea,
Mary, star of the sea,
Today he came to birth.

PART 10

The English Motet

Example 56.

Inviolata integra mater—Inviolata integra et casta (troped chant setting in single-texted three-voice motet form)

Oxford, Bodleian Lib., Lat. lit. d.20 (*Ob 20*), fols. 23′–24.

The added trope in the upper voices is shown in italics in the translation. Musical sections given between square brackets are missing in the original and have been reconstructed from analogous passages.

Example 56. *Inviolata integra mater—Inviolata integra et casta*

Example 56. *Inviolata integra mater—Inviolata integra et casta*

172

Example 56. *Inviolata integra mater—Inviolata integra et casta*

Triplum and Motetus

1a. Inviolate, whole, *without spot* and chaste,
    art thou, *O Virgin* Mary,

1b. Who art made *queen, friend of the highest King,*
    glory of the angels and the shining gate of heaven.

2a. O kind *and gracious* mother, *how fair and beautiful thou art,*
    and most dear to Christ.

2b. *Arise, O Lady, in mercy,* receive the pious offerings of praises

3a. Which now devoutly voice and heart *celebrate*
    to thy glory and entreat *thine honor,*

3b. That *both* our hearts and bodies may be *most* pure *and clean,*
    without stain of sin.

4a. Grant, *O most holy Virgin,* by thy prayers most sweet,

4b. To us, *thy servants, in the highest kingdom of heaven*
    to enjoy everlasting life.

5. O kind *and most glorious* lady.

Tenor

1a. Inviolate, whole and chaste art thou, Mary,

1b. Who art made the shining gate of heaven.

2a. O kind mother, most dear to Christ,

2b. Receive the pious offerings of praises,

3a. Which now devoutly voice and heart entreat,

3b. That our hearts and bodies may be pure.

4a. Grant by thy prayers most sweet,

4b. To us, to enjoy everlasting life,

5. O kind lady.

Example 57.
O Maria stella maris—Jhesu fili summi—
[Tenor] (double motet)

Oxford, Corpus Christe College, 497 (*Ob 497*), fol. 5(2)′–6(4).

Reference numbers in the transcription follow the tenor ordines.

Example 57. *O Maria stella maris—Jhesu fili summi*

Example 57. *O Maria stella maris—Jhesu fili summi*

Triplum

O Mary, star of the sea,
Healthful medicine
Of bodies and of hearts,
Pure font, hidden source,
Way of peace, gate of life,
Helper of the poor;
In this vale of tears,
In this place of darkness,
Against the snares of our enemies,
Guard and defend us.
Be our helper,
And bestow what is needful.

Motetus

Jesu, Son of the highest Father,
Jesu, Son of the highest Mother
And unspoiled Virgin,
Who descended from heaven
And, descending, took
The form of true man
Of thy Mother,
Mercifully deliver us from the mire,
Wash from us the dregs of sins,
And grant us a pure life,
And give us enduring peace,
And bestow salvation.

Example 58.

W. de Wycombe (Wichbury?)?, *Alleluya Christo iubilemus—Alleluya: Dies sanctificatus* (troped chant setting)

Oxford, Bodleian Lib., Rawlinson C.400* (*Ob 400*), fragments 1a/2a/3a.

A setting of a complete troped Alleluia for the third Mass of Christmas in which newly composed three-voice tropes introduce each of the Alleluia sections and the verse. Normal performance proceeds through sections 1 and 2 (the introductory trope and alleluia), sections 3 to 7 (the troped verse), and sections 8 and 9 (a second introductory trope and alleluia). However, an alternate ending is given (section 10) without the final trope, which may be used if time does not permit the singing of sections 8 and 9. The attribution to Wycombe or Wichbury is unclear.

Example 58. W. de Wycombe(?), *Alleluya Christo iubilemus—Alleluya: Dies sanctificatus*

178

Example 58. W. de Wycombe(?), *Alleluya Christo iubilemus—Alleluya: Dies sanctificatus*

Example 58. W. de Wycombe(?), *Alleluya Christo iubilemus*—*Alleluya: Dies sanctificatus*

Example 58. W. de Wycombe(?), *Alleluya Christo iubilemus—Alleluya: Dies sanctificatus*

Triplum

> *Alleluia,*
> *Let us rejoice in Christ;*
> *Let us worthily celebrate*
> *The nativity of Christ*
> *With gladness.*
> Alleluia.

> ℣ *This is the day of the sun of righteousness,*
> *The hallowed day has shone upon us,*
> *True God has truly been made flesh.*
> Come, ye people, *to offer faith,*
> *And to rejoice in Christ,*
> *And adore the Lord,*
> *For today a great light has descended with heavenly rays,*
> *The Son of the Mother gives great joys to men.*

> *Alleluia,*
> *Christ has been given to us;*
> *Let things earthly and heavenly*
> *Resound with sweet symphony;*
> *Eya, Muse, give paeans of praise of God.*
> Alleluia.

Motetus

Alleluia,
Let us rejoice in Christ;
Let us worthily celebrate the nativity of Christ;
Let the choir sing with gladness.
Alleluia.

℣ *This is the day of the sun of righteousness.*
The day is here of the new grace,
The natal day of the King of Glory,
The hallowed, *joyful* day has shone upon us
With new ray of new light,
The hallowed birthday of Christ.
Come, ye people, and adore the Lord,
For today, *the very day of God,*
On which glad praise of him is made,
A great light descended.

Alleluia,
Christ has been given unto us;
Let things heavenly and earthly
Resound with sweet symphony,
Echoing paeans of praises.
Alleluia.

Tenor

Alleluia,
Let us rejoice in Christ;
Let us worthily celebrate the nativity of Christ.
Alleluia.

℣ The hallowed day has shone upon us.
O come, ye people, and adore the Lord,
For today a great light has descended over the earth.

Alleluia,
Eya, Muse, or give paeans of praises to God.
Alleluia.

Example 59.
Dulciflua tua memoria—Precipua michi—
Tenor de Dulciflua (double motet)

Oxford, Bodliean Lib., Lat. lit. d.20 (*Ob* 20), fol. 23'.

Example 59. *Dulciflua tua memoria—Precipua michi—Tenor de Dulciflua*

185

Example 59. *Dulciflua tua memoria — Precipua michi — Tenor de Dulciflua*

Triplum

The sweet-flowing memory of thee, O Mary,
Thou royal offspring, thou wondrous mother
   of the highest king, O Mary,
The confidence of my heart, O Mary,
That thy graciousness might save me
   from the misery of sin, O Mary.

Motetus

It gives to me exceeding joy, O Mary,
Thou glory of the clergy, holy joy of virgins, O Mary.
Be thou the guardian of the memory of thee, O Mary,
Lead me to the joys which are in the gladness
   of the blessed, O Mary.

Example 60.

Solaris ardor—Gregorius sol—Petre tua— Mariounette douche (triple motet)

Oxford, New College, 362 (*Onc* 362), fol. 89.

Example 60. *Solaris ardor—Gregorius sol—Petre tua—Mariounette douche*

Example 60. *Solaris ardor—Gregorius sol—Petre tua—Mariounette douche*

A motet in honor of Saint Augustine, who came from Rome to England as a missionary in the sixth century and became the first archbishop of Canterbury. *Romulus* in the quadruplum refers to Rome, while the triplum speaks of the pope (Gregory) sending Augustine (*Jupiter*) to England (*Anglia*) in the degree (longitude and latitude) of Canterbury.

The rhythm of paired semibreves is undefined in English-style Franconian notation. They are here transcribed long-short, while Example 61 uses the short-long alternative.

Quadruplum

The warmth of the sun of Romulus
Melts the ice of Britain,
And heals the people's worldly hearts
Of the filthiness of madness,
When, with the sign-bearing comet,
The forty stars bestowed
The light of moderation
In the dawn of Kent;

Example 60. *Solaris ardor—Gregorius sol—Petre tua—Mariounette douche*

Which blazing torches of the faith
Dispelled the darkness of perfidy,
Wherever the ocean's tides today
Surround the English.

Triplum

Gregory, sun of the age,
Sent Jupiter from the Cancer of Romulus
To the Libra of Anglia;
Who took away from the people's midst
The moon of faithlessness.
Each Zodiacal sign
He crossed three times,
Shining without blemish,
And from the highest course,
He firmly fixed himself in course,
To remain forever
In the degree of Canterbury.

Motetus

Peter, your little bark
Sometimes vacillates,
But it many times recovers
After frequent perils.
In the isle of Britain,
Once the faith grew strong;
But through fear of Gentile madness,
It has long lain in hiding.
Through your successor, Gregory,
It is encouraged to endure,
And by Augustine, the monk,
It is led back into faith.

Example 61.

Ave miles celestis—Ave rex
(voice-exchange motet)

Oxford, Bodleian Lib., E.mus.7 (*Ob* 7), fol. v′–vi.

191

Example 61. *Ave miles celestis—Ave rex*

192

Example 61. *Ave miles celestis—Ave rex*

193

Example 61. *Ave miles celestis—Ave rex*

Based on the Magnificat antiphon for the Feast of Saint Edmund, king and martyr (November 20), the motet is in his honor. Each section of the antiphon is repeated in voice exchange between the two tenors, while simultaneous voice exchange occurs between the triplum and motetus. A single poem is shared by the upper voices. The tenor words are copied in red, indicating they are not to be sung, but are cues to places within the antiphon (the final *euouae* indicates a conclusion using a psalm tone *differentia*). The concluding words suggest the motet was intended as an extended *Benedicamus* trope.

Example 61. *Ave miles celestis—Ave rex*

Triplum

Hail, O soldier of the court of heaven,
Whom the honor of victory adorns;
In God you live, enjoying rest
In the manner of the holy ones.

Motetus

Hail King, patron of the homeland,
Morning light of Saxony,
Shining on us at noonday,
Star of Englishmen.

Triplum

Now you rejoice
With the citizens on high,

Motetus

Martyred Edmund,
You outshine the rest;

Triplum

Yet you do not desert your folk,
Whom you know to be devoted to you;

Motetus

You restore by prayer the footsteps of the lame,
You cleanse the leper and set the captive free.

Triplum

Your deeds confirm the faith by the telling,
The blind see, and the dead arise;

Motetus

With right judgment you keep off the enemies,
You spare your servants, with a kindly heart.

Triplum

Strengthened by the intercession of so great a king,
Let us devoutly bless the Lord.

Motetus

Make us, O martyr, at life's end,
Worthily to praise the Lord.

Example 62.

Rosa delectabilis—[Regali ex progenie]—Regalis exoritur (duet motet)

Oxford, New College, 362 (Onc 362), fols. 90′–91.

Example 62. *Rosa delectabilis — [Regali ex progenie] — Regalis exoritur*

Example 62. *Rosa delectabilis*—[*Regali ex progenie*]—*Regalis exoritur*

ma - bi - lis et gra - ci - o - sa fa - ci - es.

e - mi - tur qui vi - tam or - bi de - de - rat. Fal - so Iu -

Fit il - la ter - ri - bi - lis ve - lud a - stro - rum a - ci -

da tra - di - tur, pa - cem re - us o - mi - se -

es. Ex - or - ta con - spi - ci - tur ex re - ga -

rat. Pre - sta tu - os ex - ci - pe re - gi - na

li pro - ge - ni - e Vir - go, que di -

tu - is e - mu - lis; Con - cla - man - tes

no - sci - tur re - is spes al - ma ve - ni - e.

ac - ci - pe nos ti - bi vi - tam ser - vu - lis. Des vi -

Example 62. *Rosa delectabilis — [Regali ex progenie] — Regalis exoritur*

Example 62. *Rosa delectabilis—[Regali ex progenie]—Regalis exoritur*

Example 62. *Rosa delectabilis—[Regali ex progenie]—Regalis exoritur*

Triplum

A delightful rose arises without thorn,
This most noble queen, without fault, is born.
She who emerges as a little twig from the root of Jesse
Is the little maiden brought forth from the stalk of David.
She, fairer than the moon, arises as the dawn;
Brighter than the material sun is she perceived,
Charming and gracious is her face,
Awe-inspiring as the starry heaven.
Arisen from regal progeny is she admired,
The Virgin, who is known as hope of sinners, bountiful of grace.
In her chaste womb did she conceive the Son of God,
Whom she, lily of modesty, serves, suckling him at her breasts.
O way of wanderers, I pray, for love of thy Son,
O Virgin, be to those who pray and who despair for guilt,
Blessed mother of succor.

Motetus

The regal mother rises, soul of beauty,
Exalted by the friendship of honor.
A new flesh, restored, is seen to rise,
And from such arises, in succession, the ruler of all things.
Life is restored to earth, and Eve is saved in grace;
And to us, by her excellence, peace is restored.
The King is troubled, he is bought, who gave life to the world;
By false Judas is he betrayed; the guilty has abandoned peace.
O noble queen, deliver thy people from thy mockers,
Receive us, crying unto thee, devoting life to thee.
Grant a way to those who praise,
And a double remedy, O queen, to all who pray.
Grant to the needy, penitent for sin,
That they who bewail their guilt may be freed from punishment,
And, at the end, be citizens of heaven.

PART 11

The Continental Motet in the Fourteenth Century

Example 63.

Philippe de Vitry, *Tuba sacre—In arboris— Virgo sum* (isorhythmic motet)

Leo Schrade, *The Roman de Fauvel and the Motets of Philippe de Vitry*, Polyphonic Music of the Fourteenth Century 1 (Monaco: Éditions de l'Oiseau-lyre, 1956); reprinted by permission.

The tenor rubric states "Black notes are imperfect and red are perfect." The red notation is shown in the transcription by brackets below the tenor part, the only voice so affected.

Example 63. Philippe de Vitry, *Tuba sacre — In arboris — Virgo sum*

Example 63. Philippe de Vitry, *Tuba sacre—In arboris—Virgo sum*

Example 63. Philippe de Vitry, *Tuba sacre—In arboris—Virgo sum*

Triplum

The trumpet of holy faith, the herald of mysteries in theaters, proclaims that what reason, the root of sin, hesitates about, must be simply acknowledged and firmly believed: that necessarily God is one in three persons and three are one; that the Virgin conceived, not with the seed of a man, but by a breath of the word, herself always virgin, and bore God and man to the world. But these supernatural things, while they are all life to believers, yet in those who are indifferent to nature, reason, mastered by steps in the aforesaid, begets doubt, and divination therefore will be relied upon, and the faith through which life in the presence of divine mysteries might more clearly be possessed is always counterfeited.

Motetus

In the empery of the arbor, virginity sits happily, bearing children; faith the mediatrix. In the midst, hidden by a branch, reason, pursued by her seven clever sisters, encouraging him that he should climb; while, rather, as he presses on, the weakness of the branches is broken. Let him seek therefore the right hand of faith, or, immortalized, he will shine falsely.

Example 64.

Guillaume de Machaut, *Quant en moy—Amour et biaute—Amara valde* (isorhythmic motet)

Paris, Bib. Nat., f. frç. 1584 (*Mach A*), fols. 414'–15.

Example 64. Guillaume de Machaut, *Quant en moy—Amour et biaute—Amara valde*

207

Example 64. Guillaume de Machaut, *Quant en moy—Amour et biaute—Amara valde*

Triplum

When first to me came Love,
So very gently
Wanted he to enamor my heart,
That a glance he gave me as a present,
And very amorously
He gave me also sweet thoughts,
[And] the hope
To receive
Mercy without being refused.
But never in all my life
Did he want to give me courage;

And so he makes me desirously
Think so [much] about love
That by way of desiring,
My joy must into torment
Change, if I don't have courage.
Alas! and I cannot help it
That Love
Help
Does not want to lend me,
[Love who] in his net so cruelly
Holds me that I cannot escape.

Nor do I want to, for while waiting for
His grace, I want humbly
To suffer all these pains.
And if Love consents
That my sweet lady with the beautiful body
Call me her friend,
I know
For certain
That I shall have unending
Joy that love to a noble lover
Must give for all his travails.

But she is waiting too long,
And I love so crazily
That I do not dare ask for mercy,

For I like better living in hope
Of receiving mercy soon
Than [seeing her] refusal come to kill me.

And therefore I say, sighing:
Great folly it is to love so much
That out of a sweet thing one makes a bitter one.

Motetus

Love and perfect beauty:
My doubts [about them]
Are concealed
By [force of your] perfection

And by true desire which makes me
Love you,
Sweet heart,
Love you without end.

And while I love so nobly,
Mercy
I beg of you:
May it be granted me

Without your honor being diminished.
For I prefer thus to languish

And to die, if it pleases you,
Rather than that through me be worsened

Your honor that I desire so,
Either by deed or by thought.

Example 65.

Guillaume de Machaut, *De bon espoir—* *Puis que la douce—Speravi* (isorhythmic motet)

Paris, Bib. Nat., f. frç. 1584 (*Mach A*), fols. 417′–18.

214

Triplum

With Good Hope, Very Sweet Remembrance
And Very Sweet Thought against Desire
Good Love has often helped me,
Whenever [Desire] ran wildly over me;
For whenever Desire gripped me strongly,
Very sweetly Hope protected me,
And Remembrance showed me the beauty,
The good sense, the honor, the merit and the goodness
Of her about whom I thought amorous thoughts
[Which] came to comfort my aching heart.
Alas! now Desire assails me more than ever.
But I must painfully endure it,
For I am close to losing the comfort
Of Good Hope, which causes me discomfort;
And Remembrance makes me always think,
To make my tired heart despair,
For Grace, Love, Frankness, Loyalty, Pity, Doctrine, and Kindliness
Are, as far as I am concerned, fast asleep,
For Danger reigns over Mercy,
And my lady, whose servant I am,
Believes in Hard-Heartedness and proud Refusal,
Simply because my love and my heart
I do not want to, and cannot, separate from her at any price.
But since it cannot be otherwise,
May she do with me as she commands,
For despite her I will love her loyally.

Motetus

Since the sweet rose
Of humility does not want to bloom
Until has ripened
Mercy that I desire so,
I cannot endure [any longer],
For in me has arisen,
By an amorous desire,
An ardor beyond all measure
That Love, through his sweet pleasure,
And my desired lady,
Through her colorful beauty,
Have graciously made to enter [my heart].
But since such is their pleasure,
I want to suffer humbly
Their wish until death.

Example 66.

Anonymous, *A vous, vierge—Ad te, virgo— Regnum mundi* (isorhythmic motet)

Leo Schrade, ed., *Motets of French Provenance*, Polyphonic Music of the Fourteenth Century 5 (Monaco: Éditions de l'Oiseau-Lyre, 1968); reprinted by permission.

Example 66. Anonymous, *A vous, vierge—Ad te, virgo—Regnum mundi*

Example 66. Anonymous, *A vous, vierge*—*Ad te, virgo*—*Regnum mundi*

Example 66. Anonymous, *A vous, vierge—Ad te, virgo—Regnum mundi*

Example 66. Anonymous, *A vous, vierge—Ad te, virgo—Regnum mundi*

Triplum

You, virgin of sweetness
Whom I adore,
I want to serve from now on,
And any other foolish love
Without delay
[I want] to leave aside quite voluntarily,
And I have in my heart a great anger
And rancor,
Because I have waited so long.
Therefore to you I return
Without turning back
Or leaving,
For you carried [the child] without labor,
Without languor
Nine months and more. Saintly
You gave birth without pain
Or sadness
And without [mortal] corruption
To our Father Creator,
Savior,
Who saved us,
Who out of charity,
Out of love
Nothing but ardor
Brought us most cordially.
Therefore, virgin of valor,
In honor
Of you have I put my mind,
Strength, and vigor
Forever
To serving honestly
You, gracious flower,
For better
I could never serve;
And I will serve you, trembling,
Without fail,
Readily and willingly;
And I pray to you like a sinner:
My clamor,
My prayer, my sorrow,
Please listen to them, and on my tears
Of affliction
Look with pity;

Example 66. Anonymous, *A vous, vierge—Ad te, virgo—Regnum mundi*

And when comes that day
Of fright,
Of the horrible judgment,
Be my castle and tower
In every court
Against the mighty enemy,
Pray to our Lord,
Redeemer,
That He may save me from torment
Always [and] forever.

Motetus

To thee, O Virgin, I am crying,
To thee, I flee for refuge,
Whom to serve is my whole desire,
With all my heart, and with great love.
Treat my capricious life as a worthless vine,
Burn up my willful spirit,
Which has flown upon what is wrong,
Which abhors destruction.
Wherefore, O Mother, beseech thy holy child,
The Father and the Son,
Since he came into the exile of this earth,
Fearful of dreadful death,
May he not give me punishment,
But, at thy intercession, close me in his house of correction
Grant me, in the world to come, to see with open eye,
The child born of thee,
And to enjoy supernal glory through the ages
In the court of heaven.
Since my merits are not enough,
Let your outstanding merits fill the gap.

Example 67.

Anonymous, *Post missarum sollempni—Post missa modulamina*—Contratenor—Tenor (four-voice double motet with alternate solus tenor)

Leo Schrade, ed., *Motets of French Provenance*, Polyphonic Music of the Fourteenth Century 5, (Monaco, Éditions de l'Oiseau-Lyre, 1968); reprinted by permission.

Example 67. Anonymous, *Post missarum sollempni*—*Post missa modulamina*—Contratenor—Tenor

225

Example 67. Anonymous, *Post missarum sollempni—Post missa modulamina—*Contratenor—Tenor

Example 67. Anonymous, *Post missarum sollempni*—*Post missa modulamina*—Contratenor—Tenor

Example 67. Anonymous, *Post missarum sollempni*—*Post missa modulamina*—Contratenor—Tenor

Example 67. Anonymous, *Post missarum sollempni—Post missa modulamina*—Contratenor—Tenor

Triplum

After the solemnities of masses, after divine eulogies,

Bishop, rule your good flock by the reflection of good deeds; be concerned only for the right, and dutifully restrain the bad.

King, your crown shining with honor, control the reins of the republic, especially to be celebrated as father of the fatherland. Consider well the traditions of government, think on the lessons of history; clothe your nobles in rough linen.

Knight, do not lust after booty, receive your wages, and do not desert, nor commit dishonor in bodily disguise.

Judge, mete out equal justice to all your clients, but befriend the weak, and beware of doing injury.

Whosoever you are, think nightly after giving thanks to God.

Motetus

After the melodies of men, and the seeds of sweet words, consider your shortcomings, and do not give yourself to idle chatter; attend to books, and manners, and letters.

Merchant, buy what is useful, and do not cheat in selling; to sell justly is to weigh with precise measure.

Builder, do not be a fabricator, but a trustworthy builder; work hard with your own hands to assure the quality of the building.

Farmer, sow, reap, and prune, as is appropriate to the season, and do not spare the hardship of the body.

You who will the good, do it, after your have given thanks to God.

PART 12

The Polyphonic Song in France

Example 68.

Guillaume de Machaut, *Dame, vostre doulze viaire* (virelai)

Paris, Bibl. Nat., f. frç. 1584 (*Mach A*), fols. 486–87.

Example 68. Guillaume de Machaut, *Dame, vostre doulze viaire*

Refrain

Lady, your sweet appearance
[So] gracious
And your serene bearing [so] quiet
Make me do you service
Without wrongdoing,
[But] with a true heart, in good faith.

1. Lady, and well must I do it,
   For worry,
   Grief, pain, or adversity
   Never, while serving you, did I have;
   Rather I know
   That nothing can displease me in your service,
   And that now [serving you] must please me more,
   Without restriction,
   The more I employ myself in your service.
   For you are so gracious
   That a model
   Of all good things in you I see.

Lady, your sweet appearance
[So] gracious
And your serene bearing [so] quiet
Make me do you service
Without wrongdoing,
[But] with a true heart, in good faith.

2. Quant je remir vostre arroy
   Sans desroy
   Ou raisons maint et repaire,
   Et vo regart sans effroy,
   Si m'esjoy
   Que tous li cuers m'en esclaire;
   Car il le scet si attraire

   Par son traire
   Qu'en vous maint; et je l'ettroy.
   Si ne weillies pas deffaire
   Ceste paire,
   Dame; humblement vous en proy.

   When I observe your disposition,
   [Which is] without disarray [and]
   Where reason dwells and lives
   And your countenance free of fear,
   I rejoice so
   That all my heart lights up because of it;
   For [your grace] knows how to attract [my
      heart]

   By its attractiveness so
   That it dwells in you; and I grant it.
   May you not wish to undo
   This companionship,
   Lady, humbly I beg you.

233

Example 68. Guillaume de Machaut, *Dame, vostre doulze viaire*

Lady, your sweet appearance
[So] gracious
And your serene bearing [so] quiet
Make me do you service
Without wrongdoing,
[But] with a true heart, in good faith.

3. Car mis l'aves en tel ploy   For you have put [my heart] into such a state
    Qu'il en soy   That in itself
    N'a riens n'alleurs ne repaire,   It has nothing, nowhere to go, nowhere to dwell

    Fors en vous, et sans anoy;   Except in you, and without worry;
    N'il ottroy   Nor does it grant
    Ne quiert merci ne salaire   Or ask for mercy or recompense
    Fors que l'amour qui le maire   Except that [my] love which dominates it
    Vous appaire   May become apparent to you
    Et que tant sachiez de soy   And that you may know it so well
    Qu'il ne saroit contrefaire   That it would be unable to fake
    Son affare.   His affairs.
    C'est tout. Mon chant vous envoy.   That's all. I send you my song.

Lady, your sweet appearance
[So] gracious
And your serene bearing [so] quiet
Make me do you service
Without wrongdoing,
[But] with a true heart, in good faith.

Example 69.

Guillaume de Machaut,
Se je souspir (virelai)

Paris, Bibl. Nat., f. frç. 1584 (*Mach A*), fols. 492–92′

235

Example 69. Machaut, *Se je souspir*

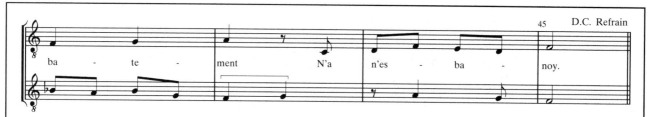

45 D.C. Refrain

ba - te - ment   N'a   n'es - ba - noy.

Refrain

If I sigh deeply
And tenderly
Cry in a hidden place,
It is, by my faith,
For you, when your beautiful, noble body,
Lady, I do not see.

1. Your sweet, simple, and quiet bearing,
   Your beautiful appearance,
   Elegant and pleasing,
   And your manners, free of fear,
   These three have taken me
   So sweetly
   That to you very amorously
   [And] entirely,
   I give and grant
   This heart of mine,
   Which far from you neither amusement
   Nor joy does have.

   If I sigh deeply
   And tenderly
   Cry in a hidden place,
   It is, by my faith,
   For you, when your beautiful, noble body,
   Lady, I do not see.

2. Si que je port plus grief anoy   And I bear more grievous worry
   Qu'onques maus n'oy,   Than ever I had,
   Secretement;   Secretly;
   Mais, par m'ame, je le conjoy   But, by my soul, I welcome
   Et le recoy   And receive it
   Tres humblement,   Very humbly,
   Que aligier poues mon tourment   Because you can alleviate my torment
   Legierement,   Gently,
   D'un seul ottray,   In one stroke,
   Et plus qu'un roy   And more than a king
   Moi faire vivre liement;   [Can you] make me live happily;
   Ansi le croy.   This I believe.

236

Example 69. Machaut, *Se je souspir*

If I sigh deeply
And tenderly
Cry in a hidden place,
It is, by my faith,
For you, when your beautiful, noble body,
Lady, I do not see.

3. Dame, mis m'aves en tel ploy,	Lady, you have put me into such a state,
Bien le percoy,	Well do I perceive it,
Que, vraiement,	That, truly,
En vous sens, temps et vie employ	In [serving you] I employ my wits, time, and life
Et toudis croy	And believe forever
En ce talent.	In this talent.
En se loing sui d'aligement	And if I am far from relief
Et povrement	And poorly
De mercy j'oy	Receive of [your] mercy,
Ne m'en desvoy,	I do not deviate [from serving you],
Car si grant honnour nullement	For such a great honor under no circumstance
Avoir ne doy.	Shall I have.

If I sigh deeply
And tenderly
Cry in a hidden place,
It is, by my faith,
For you, when your beautiful, noble body,
Lady, I do not see.

Example 70.

Guillaume de Machaut, *Puis qu'en oubli* (rondeau)

Paris, Bib. Nat., frç. 1584 (*Mach A*), fol. 480'.

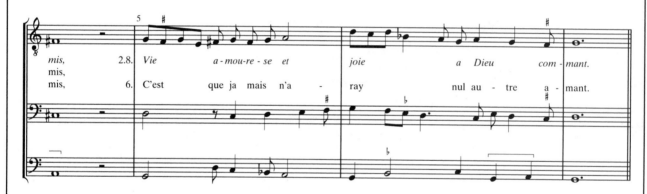

Since oblivious you are of me, sweet friend,
Amorous life and joy to God I commend.
To my misfortune was I born, since love put me in you[r thoughts],
Since oblivious you are of me, sweet friend.
But this I will keep which to you I have promised,
That is, that never will I have another lover.
Since oblivious you are of me, sweet friend,
Amorous life and joy to God I commend.

238

Example 71.
Guillaume de Machaut, *Quant je ne voy*
(rondeau)

Paris, Bib. Nat., f. frç. 22546 (*Mach G*), fols. 162–62′.

[Cantus]

1.4.7. Quant je   ne   voy
3. Mes   cuers   font   en
5. N'on - ques   tel   mal,

Contratenor

Tenor

ma   da - me
moy   com - me
par   m'a - me,

Example 71. Machaut, *Quant je ne voy*

240

Example 71. Machaut, *Quant je ne voy*

When I do not see my lady nor hear [her],
I see nothing that grieves me not.
My heart melts in me like snow,
When I do not see my lady nor hear [her].
Never such worry, by my soul, I had
For my eye, which in tears drowns me
When I do not see my lady nor hear [her],
I see nothing that grieves me not.

Example 72.

Guillaume de Machaut, *Amours me fait desirer* (ballade)

Paris, Bib. Nat., f. frç. 1584 (*Mach A*), fol. 463′.

In this and the following transcriptions, accidentals in parentheses are those which, although not present in this manuscript, are to be found in at least one other Machaut source.

Example 72. Machaut, *Amours me fait desirer*

Example 72. Machaut, *Amours me fait desirer*

1. Love makes me desirous
   And amorous;
   But it is so crazy
   That I cannot hope
   Nor think
   Nor imagine at all
   That the sweet, noble face
   That inflames me,
   Would give me joy
   Unless love acts properly
   So that
   I may have it without asking for it.

2. S'ay si dur a endurer
   Que durer
   Ne puis mie longuement;
   Car en mon cuer weil celer
   Et porter
   Ceste amour couvertement,
   Sans requerre aligement,
   Qu'a tourment
   Weil mieus ma vie finer.
   Et si n'ay je pensement
   Vraiement
   Que je l'aie sans rouver.

   And I have such hardship to endure
   That last
   I cannot long;
   For in my heart I want to conceal
   And carry
   This love covertly,
   Without requesting relief,
   Because in torment
   I prefer my life to finish.
   And I have no other thought,
   Truly, [but that]
   I may have it without asking for it.

3. Mais desirs fait embraser
   Et doubler
   Ceste amour si asprement
   Que tout m'en fait oublier,
   Ne penser
   N'ay fors a li seulement;
   Et pour ce amoureusement
   Humblement
   Langui sans joie gouster.
   S'en morray, se temprement
   Ne n'assent
   Que je l'aie sans rouver.

   My desire makes burn
   And double
   This love so violently
   That it makes me forget everything;
   Not a thought
   I have except for it.
   And therefore amorously,
   Humbly,
   I languish without tasting joy.
   And I will die of it, if soon
   It does not consent to [my wish that]
   I may have it without asking for it.

Example 73.

Guillaume de Machaut, *Une vipere en cuer*
(ballade)

Paris, Bib. Nat., f. frç. 9221 (*Mach E*), fol. 148.

245

Example 73. Machaut, *Une vipere en cuer*

Example 73. Machaut, *Une vipere en cuer*

1. A viper in her heart my lady carries,
   Which plugs with its tail her ear,
   So that she may not hear my painful lament;
   Of that [and] nothing else it is forever watchful and tends its ear.
   And in her mouth sleeps
   The scorpion that stings my heart to death;
   A basilisk she has in her sweet glance.
   These three have killed me and she whom God may keep.

2. Quant en plourant li depri qu'elle m'aint,
   Desdains ne puet souffrir que oïr me weille,
   Et s'alle en croit mon cuer, quant il se plaint,
   En sa bouche Refus pas ne sommeille,
   Ains me point au cuer trop fort;
   Et son regart prent deduitet deport,

   Quant mon cuer voit font et frit et art.

   Cil troy m'ont mort et elle que Dieus gart.

   When crying I implore her to love me,

   Disdain cannot suffer her hearing me,

   And if she believes my heart when it complains,

   In her mouth Refusal is not asleep,
   But stings me in my heart very strongly;
   And her glance robs me of joy and happiness

   When she sees my heart which melts and fries and burns.

   These three have killed me and she whom God may keep.

3. Amours, tu sces qu'elle m'a fait mal maint
   Et que siens suy toudis, weille ou ne weille.
   Mais quant tu fuis et Loyaute se faint
   Et Pitez n'a talent qu'elle s'esveille,
   Je n'i voy si bon confort
   Com tost morir; car en grant desconfort.

   Desdains, Refus, regars qui mon cuer art.

   Cil troy m'ont mort et elle que Dieus gart.

   Love, you know that she has treated me badly

   And that I am hers always, whether she likes it or not.

   But when you flee and Loyalty faints
   And Pity has no intention of waking up,
   I see no other comfort
   Than to die right away; for in great discomfort

   I observe Disdain and Refusal who inflame my heart.

   These three have killed me and she whom God may keep.

Example 74.
Guillaume de Machaut, *De toutes flours* (ballade)

Paris, Bib. Nat., f. frç. 9221 (*Mach E*), fol. 150'.

248

Example 74. Machaut, *De toutes flours*

249

Example 74. Machaut, _De toutes flours_

1. Of all flowers and of all fruits there was
   In my garden but a single rose:
   Ravaged had been the rest and destroyed
   By fortune, who is cruelly opposed
   To this sweet flower
   In order to dull its color and its odor.
   But if I see it being picked or drooping,
   Another one after it never I wish to have.

2. Mais vraiement ymaginer ne puis
   Que la vertus, ou ma rose est enclose,

   Viengne par toy et par tes faus conduis,

   Ains est drois dons natureus; si suppose

   Que tu n'avras ja vigour
   D'amanrir son pris et sa valour.
   Lay la moy donc, qu'alleurs n'en mon
   vergier
   Autre apres li ja mais avoir ne quier.

   But truly I cannot imagine
   That the virtue in which my rose is en-
   closed
   Derives from you, [Fortune,] and from
   your false conduct;
   Rather [this rose] is a rightful, natural
   gift; and I suppose
   That you will never have the vigor
   To lessen its price and its valor.
   Let me keep it, then, for neither
   elsewhere nor in my garden
   Another one after it never I wish to have.

3. He! Fortune, qui es gouffres et puis

   Pour engloutir tout homme qui croire
   ose,
   Ta fausse loy, ou riens de biens ne truis

   Ne de seūr, trop est decevans chose;

   Ton ris, ta joie, t'onnour
   Ne sont que plour, tristesse et
   deshonnour.
   Se ty faus tour font ma rose sechier,
   Auter apres li ja mais avoir ne quier.

   Hey! Fortune, [you] who are a pit and a
   well
   Swallowing up any man who dares to
   believe,
   Your false law, in which I find nothing
   good
   And nothing sure, is a very deceiving
   thing;
   Your laughter, your joy, your honor
   Are but tears, sadness, and dishonor.

   If your false tricks make my rose dry up,
   Another one after it never I wish to have.

Example 75.

Jacob Senleches, *Fuions de ci*
(ballade in mannerist style)

Willi Apel, *French Secular Music of the Late Fourteenth Century*, (Cambridge, Mass.: The Medieval Academy of America, 1950); reprinted by permission.

Example 75. Jacob Senleches, *Fuions de ci*

252

Example 75. Jacob Senleches, *Fuions de ci*

o - nor.

A personal lament on the death of Senleches's patroness, Eleanor, Queen of Aragon, in 1382.

1. Let's flee from here, let's flee, poor companion,
   May everyone go look for his adventure
   In Aragon, in France, or in Britanny,
   For in a short time one will no longer worry about us,
   Let's flee and look for a secure life,
   We will not stay here [another] hour or day,
   For we have lost Alionor.

2. Car c'est bien drois, Rayson le nous emseigne,
   Puisque la mort tres cruel et obscure
   Nous a osté la royone d'Espaingne
   Nostre maestresse ou confort et mesure.
   Que chascuns ovre leur volunté pure
   De bien briefment vuidier de ce contour,
   Puis que perdu avons Alionor.

   For it is quite right, Reason teaches it to us,
   Since very cruel and obscure death
   Has taken from us the queen of Spain,
   Our mistress, comfort and guide,
   That everybody exercise his pure will
   To leave very quickly this region,
   For we have lost Alionor.

3. Mais au partir persoune ne se faingne
   Que de bon cuer et loialté seüre
   Ne prie Dieux que l'ame de li preingne,
   Et qu'elle n'est sa penitence dure,
   Mais paradis qui de jour en jour dure.
   Et puis pensons d'aler sans nul sojor,
   Puis que perdu avons Alionor.

   But that upon leaving nobody [simply] pretend
   With good heart and pure loyalty
   To be praying to God that He take her soul,
   And that she not receive her hard penitence,
   But [rather] paradise, which lasts forever!
   And then let's think of traveling without rest,
   For we have lost Alionor.

253

PART 13

The Polyphonic Song in Italy

Example 76.

Giovanni da Firenze, *Appress' un fiume*
(madrigal)

Florence, Bibl. Nazionale Centrale, Panciatichi 26 (*F1*), fol. 50'.

Example 76. Giovanni da Firenze, *Appress' un fiume*

Example 76. Giovanni da Firenze, *Appress' un fiume*

One of six madrigals (two each) written by Giovanni, Jacopo da Bologna, and Magister Piero in a musical rivalry honoring the unidentified "Anna," presumably a lady associated with the court of Mastino della Scala in Verona.

Close by a clear river
Ladies and maidens danced around
A tree adorned with lovely flowers.

Among them, I saw one,
Fair and courteous and tender,
Who moved me with sweet song.

ANNA, *to love your courteous*
   countenance inspires me,
The sweet glance and the elegant hand.

Example 77.
Lorenzo Masini da Firenze, *Sovra la riva* (madrigal)

Florence, Bibl. Nazionale Centrale, Panciatichi 26 (*F1*), fols. 75′–76.

Example 77. Lorenzo Masini da Firenze, *Sovra la riva*

Example 77. Lorenzo Masini da Firenze, *Sovra la riva*

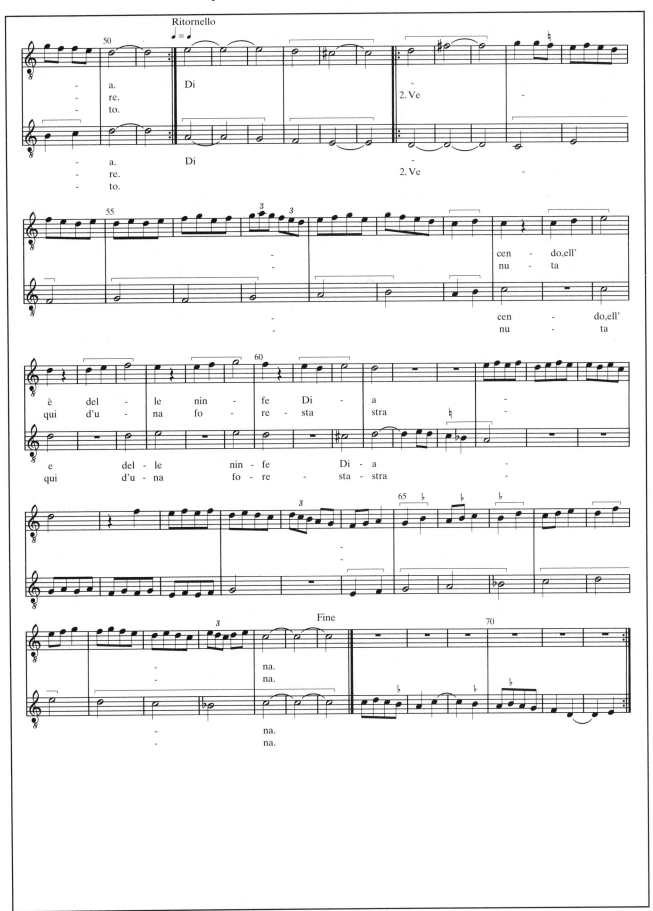

Example 77. Lorenzo Masini da Firenze, *Sovra la riva*

On the bank of the running stream,
Love moved me, when I heard a song.
Without knowing from what mouth it came.

It gave such delight unto my heart,
That I turned to my master to inquire
From what source came such sweet desire

And, as a kind master, he enlightened me,
And with his finger pointed to
A lady singing, sitting on a couch;

Saying, "She is one of Diana's nymphs,
Who has come here from a strange forest."

Example 78.
Giovanni da Firenze, *Chon brachi assai* (caccia)

Florence, Bibl. Nazionale Centrale, Panciatichi 26 (*F1*), fol. 92′.

263

Example 78. Giovanni da Firenze, *Chon brachi assai*

Example 78. Giovanni da Firenze, *Chon brachi assai*

Example 78. Giovanni da Firenze, *Chon brachi assai*

Example 78. Giovanni da Firenze, *Chon brachi assai*

A caccia with two stanzas in the main section. The same text was set by Magister Piero in an apparent continuation of the musical rivalry noted in Example 76. The reference to the river Adda places the composition in the environs of Milan.

With plenty of hounds and many hawks
We hunted birds on the banks of the Adda;
And one cried,
"Go! Go!"
And another,
"Over here, Varin,
Come back, Picciolo!"
Others took the quail on the wing,
When a great rainstorm came.

No greyhound ever coursed o'er a field
As we all did, to flee the rain;
And one cried,
"Here now!
Give me my coat!"
And another,
"Give me my hat!"
When I found shelter with my hawk,
There a shepherdess pierced my heart.

She was alone there, whence I said to myself,
"Here is the rain, here are Dido and Aeneas."

Example 79.
Francesco Landini, *I' priego amor* (ballata)

Florence, Bib. Laur., Palatino 87 (*Sq*), fol. 162.

Example 79. Francesco Landini, *I' priego amor*

Example 79. Francesco Landini, *I' priego amor*

Example 79. Francesco Landini, *I' priego amor*

I beseech love and thy beauty
To pity my distress.

Proud honor and fair elegance in countenance
Nature shaped in thee with all her power.
The only hope of my wretched soul,
By serving well, to find reward in such a creature.
How wrong that such a noble beauty
Should be veiled by scorn and cruelty.

I beseech love and thy beauty
To pity my distress.

Example 80.

Francesco Landini, *Cara mie donna*
(ballata)

Florence, Bib. Laur., Palatino 87 (*Sq*), fol. 161.

Example 80. Francesco Landini, *Cara mie donna*

273

Example 80. Francesco Landini, *Cara mie donna*

Example 80. Francesco Landini, *Cara mie donna*

O lady dear to me, henceforth I live content,
For rather will I suffer my great pain
With your full approval
Than seek solace for the desire which tortures me.

I must seek solace from you,
From that pleasure which disturbs your mind,
Which I cannot have unless you give it,
For with suffering the heart sympathizes.
But I love you so perfectly
That, while I long for the gift of yourself,
Yet in my heart I am content,
Knowing that you are not content to give it.

O lady dear to me, henceforth I live content,
For rather will I suffer my great pain
With your full approval
Than seek solace for the desire which tortures me.